"Many men sense an uncertainty about where their life is going and how they got to where they are. Mark Elfstrand helps men to identify 10 passions common to us and lets us know how these passions are key to living life to its fullest."

Doug Haugen, Director
Lutheran Men in Mission

"Mark has written a fine book that captures with practicality and personal transparency the resolute strength indicative of a passionate man. This book is more than 10 concepts. It mines the depths of a man's soul, the inner vault of God's investment . . . masculinity."

Preston Gillham
Author, Speaker, Consultant, and President
Lifetime Guarantee, Inc. and Gillham Consulting.com

"Mark does an outstanding job of dissecting the 10 passions that drive a man, giving the reader concrete principles upon which to understand our masculinity and get it in balance with God's designed role for men. I highly recommend this read for every man who cares about being one of God's best men."

Jim Cote
Founder & President
The Master's Men

10 Passions of a Man's Soul

Mark Elfstrand

MOODY PUBLISHERS

CHICAGO

© 2006 by
MARK ELFSTRAND

All Scripture quotations, unless otherwise indicated, are taken from the *Holy Bible, New International Version®*. NIV®. Copyright © 1973, 1978, 1984 by International Bible Society. Used by permission of Zondervan Publishing House. All rights reserved.

Scripture quotations marked TLB are taken from *The Living Bible* copyright © 1971. Used by permission of Tyndale House Publishers, Inc., Wheaton, Illinois 60189. All rights reserved.

Scripture quotations marked THE MESSAGE are from *The Message*, copyright © by Eugene H. Peterson 1993, 1994, 1995. Used by permission of NavPress Publishing Group.

Scripture quotations marked NASB are taken from the *New American Standard Bible®*, copyright © 1960, 1962, 1963, 1968, 1971, 1972, 1973, 1975, 1977, 1995 by The Lockman Foundation. Used by permission.

Scripture quotations marked NLT are taken from the *Holy Bible, New Living Translation*, copyright © 1996. Used by permission of Tyndale House Publishers, Inc., Wheaton, Illinois 60189, U.S.A. All rights reserved.

Cover Design: Paetzold Associates
Cover Image: Getty Images
Editor: Jim Vincent

ISBN: 0-8024-0866-4
ISBN-13: 978-0-8024-0866-2

Library of Congress Cataloging-in-Publication Data

Elfstrand, Mark.
    10 passions of a man's soul / Mark Elfstrand.
        p. cm.
    Includes bibliographical references.
    ISBN-13: 978-0-8024-0866-2
        1. Christian men—Religious life. 2. Masculinity—Religious aspects—Christianity.
I. Title. II. Title: Ten passions of a man's soul.

BV4528.2.E54 2006
248.8'42--dc22

                                                                    2006014341

We hope you enjoy this book from Moody Publishers. Our goal is to provide high-quality, thought-provoking books and products that connect truth to your real needs and challenges. For more information on other books and products written and produced from a biblical perspective, go to www.moodypublishers.com or write to:

Moody Publishers
820 N. LaSalle Boulevard
Chicago, IL 60610

1 3 5 7 9 10 8 6 4 2

Printed in the United States of America

To my sons, Marshall and Adam,
and to my son-in-law, Andy Williames.
May these pages inspire and encourage you . . .
and many other men as well.

Contents

Foreword

"All they wanted was their chance to be men . . . and he gave it to them." That's the clever tagline for a classic western film, *The Cowboys*. Considered by many to be one of John Wayne's greatest movies, it is the tale of an aging cattle rancher, Wil Anderson, who needs to get his herd to town. Unfortunately, all the able-bodied men who could help him in that work are off chasing visions of gold. So Anderson decides to hire on a ragtag bunch of eleven boys, ages nine to fifteen.

While these youngsters know nearly nothing about the work of being a cowboy, they know even less about being a man. The film offers an entertaining and instructive look at what manhood is all about.

After the climactic close of the DVD, my sons and I had some conversations about the themes of honor, courage, justice, and redemption. In the story that group of boys had to face some tough questions about life and themselves, like "What am I doing here? Do I have what it takes to be a man? Are we gonna make it through this?"

Today we see a disturbing lack of understanding about real manhood. One reason is a lack of good role models. More and more young men grow up in fatherless homes, without the benefit of masculine influence. Statistically, boys who grow up fatherless have troubles, and lots of them: poor self-esteem, challenges in school, a tendency to violence. They often lack an ability to relate well to others. There is sometimes gender confusion.

We also suffer from a lack of vision as to what a man is and how he should act. Think about the (unfortunate) stereotypes of men in film and on television. Unlike the characters in *The Cowboys,* today men are typically portrayed in the media as dumb, insensitive, unmotivated brutes who are only interested in indulging their passions. Those passions? Why, sex, drinking beer, making money, and breaking things. And that's about it. Is that really all that manhood is about?

You and I know that Christian men are not immune to these challenges. Knowing Jesus does not insulate us from the struggles of the male life. We want to know real masculinity, have personal meaning, and find fulfillment living life with purpose. Witness the explosion of conferences, books, videos, and other resources addressing biblical manhood. There is a hunger for answers.

If you yourself have searched for those answers, I think you'll appreciate this book. It should prove to be an excellent guide for your journey in becoming a more godly man.

In these pages my friend Mark Elfstrand speaks with clarity and transparency. He offers biblical and historical insights about real manhood. He also has included personal insights from some men who have that "been there" experience from which we can so easily learn.

The author doesn't preach down to the reader. He isn't perfect, as you'll read in these pages. He's had his share of difficulties and challenges in life. And I think his humility and heart make for a powerful resource.

As my wife and I have endeavored to raise our sons to be good young men, a recurring prayer has been this: "God, cultivate within them a heart that pleases You." I want them to have a confidence about who they are and how God has uniquely gifted them. I want them to possess a righteous zeal for life, for making an impact in others, for authentic living. Oh, that they would live like King David, whose heart and passions were for his God!

Before my boys leave our home, I plan to share the concepts and stories in this book with them. And we'll probably watch *The Cowboys* one more time, too.

JOHN FULLER
Cohost of Focus on the Family radio broadcasts

Acknowledgments

This material was "field tested" with the BraveHearts men of Grace Pointe Church in Naperville, Illinois. Special thanks to Tom Cole, Jim Rempel, Dale Bates, Jim Rabe, Ben Mammina, and Mick DiSanto who assisted me so faithfully. I am also grateful to Mark Williames for his technical expertise.

Grace Pointe's senior pastor, John Bell, encouraged me to pursue the development of this material while I served on staff as director of men's ministries. John was always an inspiration to me and has a heart for men.

In addition, I thank all of the men at Grace Pointe who were faithful in participating in the Ten Passions series.

Finally, I am grateful for several influential men in my life: Arthur Elfstrand, Glenn Murray, Rick Irwin, and Gene Quinn.

Introduction My Passion for Men's Lives

My passion for men dates back to the late 1980s and Gordon Dalbey's classic book on manhood, *Healing the Masculine Soul*. It opened my eyes as to how widespread the problem of authentic manhood was among men of my generation.

Women's liberation had brought men a new term: male chauvinist pigs. Ouch! I didn't think I was one of them but I did see that there was a difference in roles that men and women should live out in response to their families. And I did believe that men should be leaders in their homes. So . . . maybe I *was* one of them!

Within a year or so after reading that book, I came across one of the best resources for men I have ever found. It is Patrick Morley's bestselling book, *The Man in the Mirror*, which is subtitled, "Solving the 24 Problems Men Face." As I read through it, I found myself identifying with almost all of what Morley wrote. It is still one of my favorites today.

More recently I served part time as director of men's ministry in a Chicago area church. That first year, we held a retreat led by Pres Gillham, author of *Things Only Men Know*. Women often joked that with that title, it must be a really *short* book . . . but his closing message had a deep impact.

Due to another commitment, I was unable to attend the final two sessions. But hearing about the response, the next day I asked Pres to lunch. "So what did you do for the last session?"

"Well, we've been talking about men and their purpose and issues like that. I got to the point where I said, 'You know, there are men in this room who have not really made the transition into manhood.' I decided to ask the men in the room to stand if they would like to make this night the night they were welcomed into the ranks of men."

"So what happened?" I asked, thinking guys in their thirties, forties, and fifties would not be moved.

"Each time I ask that, I feel really stupid because I think, 'Nobody is going to respond to this.' But what happened with your men, Mark, is about the same that happens each time I do this. About half of the men in the room stood up."

I almost fell off my chair. Pres Gillham was hitting a nerve.

So what was it that men needed to make this psychological adjustment to manhood? How prevalent was this among all men? And did resources exist to help provide men with the tools to do something about it?

The following year I found one answer. My pastor, a church elder, and I met with Dr. Robert Lewis, the founder of Men's Fraternity and teacher of the video series, The Quest for Authentic Manhood. We attended one of his live training sessions, dialogued with Dr. Lewis privately, and then adapted his material as part of a series for our own men. We announced that we had a new course on how to achieve authentic manhood.

The first week, more than 100 men showed up. The second week, we edged closer to 150. We videotaped the presentations of our pastor, and I then hosted a second session on Saturday mornings, using the video. A different group of forty men attended faithfully. Men's ministry hit a new peak. It was very exciting.

The following year, we used another series from Men's Fraternity called "The Great Adventure." We were still reaching more than 120 men per week. More importantly, we were giving them valuable, life-changing information. Our men were becoming authentic men!

Through these books, materials and experience, I had gained a much clearer sense of what interested and attracted men. And I was much more confident I could put my finger on *what drives a man most.*

I then developed a second course for our men consisting of all new material called "The Ten Passions of Manhood." I sought input from well-established ministry leaders around the United States. My radio work gives me access to lots of gifted people, and I wanted to get their ideas on these passions. At the end of each chapter, you can read the thoughts of such people as Bill McCartney, John Eldredge, Dr. Joe Stowell, Dr. Gary Chapman, and others. All have experience in touching the lives of men.

The Ten Passions of Manhood turned out to be a valuable course for our men. It further verified for me that men want to be men. They want to identify with manhood. They want to connect relationally with other men.

In each of the series we presented, the teaching portion was followed up with small-group discussion. Some guys jump into discussion in the small group. They love to interact with other men and share their lives. Other guys take a while. They're not even too sure they ought to be meeting with three guys privately without their wives present. So it's a process.

Like the course, this book will offer you an in-depth look at ten of the driving forces in men's lives—passions that are common to all men. Second, each chapter will help you to develop an understanding as to how a man gets out of balance in these passions and how to get back on course.

Two kinds of people probably will read *10 Passions of a Man's Soul*: men . . . and women. If you are a woman curious enough to read about the passions that drive a man, I pray you'll understand us a bit better.

If you're a guy, I hope this book will challenge you to appreciate manhood and all that God designed it to be.

This book is designed to help men be men. It is intended as a practical resource with personal stories, takeaways, and principles upon which to build your life. May it inspire you to be all that God created you to be and truly live . . . as a man!

Many people have a wrong idea of what constitutes true happiness. It is not attained through self-gratification, but through fidelity to a worthy purpose.

—Helen Keller

And don't be wishing you were someplace else or with someone else. Where you are right now is God's place for you. Live and obey and love and believe right there.

—1 Corinthians 7:17 (THE MESSAGE)

1 The Passion for Purpose

With more than 24 million copies sold of his blockbuster *The Purpose-Driven Life*, Rick Warren is somewhat of an expert on our need for purpose. During an interview on CNN's *Larry King Live*, he admitted that knowing our purpose in life is crucial yet challenging: "I think everybody wants to know their purpose in life. If you read most self-help books, they fundamentally will say things like, 'Make up your purpose. Figure out your purpose. Look for your purpose.' And the big one is, 'Look within.' It's kind of like, 'Trust the force, Luke.' You know, 'Look within.'

"When I looked within, I didn't like what I saw. You know, I just got confused. The truth is, I didn't create me, so I can't tell me what my purpose is."

I can understand his confusion now. But when I graduated from high school, I thought I knew my future, including my purpose. I sure wasn't looking within.

On graduation night, some buddies and I went up to a hilltop just outside Sidney, Montana, located on the border with North Dakota. That June, 1969, night was an exciting time . . . and a turbulent time!

During my four years in high school, there were two assassinations (a third American leader, President John Kennedy, was assassinated just a couple years before I entered high school), the Vietnam war, and hippies, who said the answers could be found in "free love" and mind-tripping drugs.

A Career Path . . . and the Quest for Purpose

Now on that hilltop, I felt pretty free and good about my future. While on the high school debate team, I wrestled with so many of the cultural issues of that period, which were capsulized in stimulating debate topics. A pretty fair debater, I had set my course to be a lawyer after graduation.

Lawyers are protectors and defenders of justice. It seemed like a noble kind of work, although now I realize there are more jokes about lawyers than just about any other profession. (You know, like why do they bury lawyers at ten feet? Because deep down they're really nice guys.)

The other career path I entertained was politics. Ironically, politicians are the group that likely ranks second in the joke business. For example: How can you tell if a politician is lying? Answer: If his lips are moving. Ouch! For better or worse, those were my primary career choices as a high school graduate . . . politics and law.

Celebrating graduation night in Sidney was probably similar to senior celebrations at a thousand other towns across America in 1969. We congregated where kids would hang out, away from their parents and responsibilities. Some of the guys had decided to "party" all night, but a lot of us simply wanted to stay up and watch the sunrise while enjoying the fact that school was over and summer was at hand. It was a magical kind of experience.

During those overnight hours, I remember comments like, "Wow! Isn't this great? We've got the whole world in front of us! How are we going to change it?" OK, we were just kids from Sidney, Montana. What would we know about changing the world, right? However, we were groomed to be idealists; our culture told us to believe our job was to create a better world.

I also remember thinking about *my role* in making a better world. Or at least my personal success. Was I going on to become a famous lawyer? A well-respected politician? Was the presidency even a possibility??? Why not? Yes, there were deep questions to ponder: What is my role in this world? What is my destiny?

Twelve Years Later . . .

Let's fast forward twelve years. I wasn't a lawyer. I had dropped out of college after several years of night classes. I was married with two children and one more on the way. It was October 1981; I had just turned thirty years old. I had a mortgage and found myself working in radio.

That year, my thirtieth birthday turned out to be what I would call my "bad birthday." It varies from man to man as to when that bad birthday hits. For some men it's forty; for others it's fifty. Whenever it hits you, be assured: A sense of crisis looms that in some way seems a bit overwhelming. The fundamental question that arises is: What happened to my life?

For me, that question arose at age thirty. All through my twenties it seemed as though I was ready and raring to change direction and go where the excitement was. But now I began to ask, "Was I supposed to grow up somewhere along the line here?" There were other thoughts. "Am I pursuing what I am supposed to be pursuing? Is this what life is all about?" It was as though I now had to get serious about the "business" called life.

Let's skip forward ten years, to October 1991. I'm now forty and have three young children and a portion of the national debt. I'm about to move to Pittsburgh in response to what I sensed is a *call* from God on my life.

I didn't know it quite then, but I was closing in on the answers to three important questions of purpose. Number one, Did I miss my calling? Number two, Have I accomplished my purpose? And number three, Am I using the gifts with which I was endowed?

Components of Purpose

Let's back up a minute. There's a lot of talk about "purpose" these days, but we need to break down that lofty word. I divide purpose into four components. (Indeed, we will look at the components of each of these ten passions.) They are: an ambition, a duty, a calling, and a cause.

Ambition

Ambition is what a man aspires to be. This is where most men spend most of their time. Whether they're aware of it or not, a man's primary focus is to do something that raises himself on the food chain of human endeavor . . . to climb the ladder by striving to succeed. He believes such ambition gives a man the sense of significance that he desires in his life.

I have a friend who somehow received an invitation to attend a function at the home of a very well-known actress. As I recall, he knew the actress when he was growing up. My friend made an interesting observation about spending time in the midst of "star personalities." He said that at the party all was well as long as the stars had attention. But if that attention faded, they would go someplace else to get that attention!

The same is true with us. When we're doing something we feel is important and don't get recognized or don't feel appreciated, we look elsewhere for that recognition. Lack of appreciation is one major reason why people change jobs.

Duty

The second component of purpose is *duty*. The "duty" to which I am referring is the list of various demands on a man that lead to noble ends. What are some common duties of man? We're to be responsible citizens. We're to be good husbands and fathers. We're supposed to be dependable coworkers or maybe leaders in the workplace. These are common duties that each man is expected to fulfill.

There is another kind of duty beyond those basics. We might call it serving mankind. This is where you reach out to help neighbors and friends. During the Great Chicago Fire, over three hundred men and women lost their lives. People were scrambling for self-preservation, but there are many accounts of men who risked their own lives in order to help others.

A third kind of duty is duty to our nation. Thousands of men and women are serving our country right now. Most serve in the military because they believe in the cause of freedom. They serve with a deep sense of purpose. I served in the U.S. Air Force. My service time was forced upon me because of a military draft. However, once I enlisted and went for training, I was able to see the bigger picture of the contributions of military service. Though I'm an air force guy, I've met many marines; I can't recall ever meeting a marine who failed to understand the importance of duty to our country.

Calling

In this passion called purpose, a key component is *calling*—that role that you are uniquely gifted to fulfill. Among the most challenging of questions for men is, "Did I miss my calling?" Knowing the answer helps a man understand his purpose.

If God is calling you into some kind of work and you are His chosen servant, He will make His calling known to you in unmistakable ways. Take Moses, for example. God spoke to him through a burning bush, and that bush got his attention. If a burning bush starts to talk to you, I recommend you listen. Who did God want? He specifically wanted Moses.

Another man described in the Bible is persecuting followers of Jesus and heads to Damascus with letters to deal harshly with even more Christians. But en route, he is struck by a blinding light and falls to the ground. There, his face pressed against the warm sand, he hears a voice from the heavens saying, "Saul, Saul, why do you persecute me?" At the same time he goes blind. The voice instructs him to get up, go to a nearby city, and meet a man who could help him. Then Saul's sight will be restored (Acts 9:4–8, 11).

It happens just as God says (Acts 9:17–19). Why? Because God was *calling* Saul (see verses 15–17).

> *Purpose serves as a principle around which to organize our lives.*
> ■ Anonymous

How about you? Anything like that happen in your lifetime? Maybe not a blinding light, but a clear signal? If so, obey and accept God's guidance. If it hasn't happened, that's a good indication that you haven't missed a specific and direct calling from God.

There is another kind of calling. You may know guys who, from the time they were relatively young, knew exactly what they wanted to do in life. It started early . . . perhaps in the teens or possibly even before. These are guys who said, "I'm going to be a lawyer." Or, "I'm going to be a surgeon." Maybe it was a fireman . . . or a photographer . . . or a fisherman. It is like an unmistakable imprint woven into their soul. They *know* what they want to do.

If so, thank God. Many men won't have that certainty. I didn't. Recall that on graduation night in Montana, I thought I might become a lawyer or a politician. Then a little bit later I got into radio and that was my focus. A few years later I got out of radio and into sales and marketing. Then back to radio; then out of radio again. Only near my fortieth birthday did I begin to understand my *professional purpose*.

God had wired me in a certain way and gifted me uniquely to be able to do something. But I had to figure out how to use it!

So if you weren't directly called by God, and you didn't have a deep sense of specific job direction, where does that leave you? Most likely, God has freed you up to choose what you'd like to do. If you haven't been given the "mission envelope," you have the beauty of choosing. Now it's up to you to determine what it is you want to do. That's an important question to answer because it will most certainly affect your sense of purpose.

Cause

The fourth component of purpose is *a cause*. This is purposeful giving of your life to something that lasts. Few men are living their lives at this level. But it is a beautiful thing to behold.

Cause-driven men are able to transcend the visible things of this world. Their pursuits are not for the temporal but for things that endure. They realize that there is more to live for than this life. They might be idealists. Many in ministry and true public-service positions are in this camp.

For a man to connect deeply with his purpose, the most critical missing piece is what motivates him. When the underlying motivations behind his work are based on serving others and fulfilling a deeper call to honor God in what he does, a man will have a meaningful purpose. Many men involve themselves in community relations activities to satisfy this basic need to make a difference. But this need should be met in the kind of work we do as well.

A few years ago I led a business seminar called "At the Top of Your Game." I began by asking this question: "When you think of a noble profession, what comes to mind?" I then asked participants to identify *one* person who they believed lived a truly noble life—a life that truly made a difference.

I presented this seminar several times, and the same name came up repeatedly: Mother Teresa. People admired her mission work in

Calcutta. To work with the "poorest of the poor" children in wretched conditions is certainly commendable. To devote a lifetime to this and build the ministry that exists today is remarkable. She lived a life of sacrifice. Though she died in 1997, her Missionaries of Charity continue to minister to the poor in Calcutta and around the world.

But then I issued a challenge. "Suppose," I said, "that I had visited the mission in Calcutta while Mother Teresa was still alive. While there, I overhear a conversation between Mother Teresa and a young nun. The young nun says, 'Mother Teresa, I so admire you. You are such an inspiration to me. I cannot believe what a life of service you have lived. You must be a great person of compassion.'

'Oh my dear, that's not why I did this,' Mother Teresa replies. 'I was a relatively unknown person, and I wanted to establish a reputation for myself. So I determined that if I went to a city like Calcutta and started a mission for children, they might even make me a saint.'"

Within the room, people chuckled a bit. I knew what they were thinking. If it was discovered that the only reason behind Mother Teresa's actions was selfish motivation for fame, it would totally change the perspective of her work. In other words, when the underlying motivation is genuine concern for human beings, we admire people and consider the work noble. If the same activity is done for purely selfish reasons, the value of that work diminishes . . . greatly.

Similarly, regardless of the kind of work you perform during your life, it will have significant purpose *only* if the motivation is to be of service to others.

When you begin with the understanding that *all* work is meant to serve others and your heart is motivated by that cause, your work takes on new meaning. Whether that role is fast-food service or corporate leadership or anything in between, you can find purpose and meaning in your work only when you see it as it was designed to be: serving others.

The famous nineteenth-century English pastor Charles Spurgeon gave us outstanding perspective on this issue:

Take care . . . that you do not forsake the path of duty by leaving your occupation, and take care you do not dishonour your profession while in it. Think little of yourselves, but do not think too little of your callings. Every lawful trade may be sanctified by the gospel to noblest ends.

Turn to the Bible, and you will find the most menial forms of labour connected either with most daring deeds of faith, or with persons whose lives have been illustrious for holiness. Therefore be not discontented with your calling. Whatever God has made your position, or your work, abide in that, unless you are quite sure that he calls you to something else.

Let your first care be to glorify God to the utmost of your power where you are. Fill your present sphere to his praise, and if he needs you in another he will show it to you. This evening lay aside vexatious ambition, and embrace peaceful content.[1]

The Purpose Continuum

Each of the ten passions has a continuum; the man of balance will be in the middle of this "balance beam" rather than at the extreme ends. Let's examine the continuum of purpose to recognize where the balance point is and whether a man is out of balance.

At one end of the purpose continuum, on the left side, is the purposeless man. This is the man who goes to work day in and day out, but he only sees his work as "a job." There is not a noble connection to his work. He does not see his unique design as a contributor. His life seems without purpose. A lot of men live like this, out of balance.

On the other end of our continuum is *the driven man*. His purpose, rightly or wrongly contrived, is to build his own empire. He allows nothing to get in his way. The driven man is in relentless pursuit. At

The Purpose Continuum

The Purposeless Man   **The Driven Man**

In Balance

hard-core levels, he is not just resolved or persistent, he becomes stubborn, unrelenting, obsessed. Occasionally, you hear the term *hell-bent.* He can become single-minded in focus, and that focus is his work. Unchecked, the driven man will burn himself out along with many others. He will lose relationships and perspective on what life is all about. His tenacity toward his mission will become his downfall.

I believe every man shows up on this continuum somewhere between purposeless living and selfish ambition.

Now, let's put a center point in that continuum, a center marker that would describe a life in balance. Such a man is *purpose centered.* That's where a man should be.

The purpose-centered man identifies how he is meeting the needs of others in what he does. He goes to work knowing that God has equipped him for his work and is using him to make the world a better place. He honors God with his attitude and his effort.

Are there men who actually live like this? I believe there are. Anytime we put others on a pedestal we risk a bit. Yet we also need heroes and role models who are living examples of the virtues worth pursuing in life. For each of our ten passions, I will identify a couple of men who certainly appear to be these examples—either by their lives or by acts they perform. Most are living; some remain vibrant models of manhood though they are no longer with us.

Manhood Models

For the passion of purpose, I believe a good example is *Henry Crowell,* the founder of Quaker Oats. While growing up in Cleveland, Henry watched as tuberculosis seemed to stalk his family. His father died of the disease when Henry (Harry) was a young boy. At age eighteen, Harry returned from prep school and discovered that he also had the early signs of tuberculosis. The doctors suggested a drier climate and Harry moved out west. It was key to his recovery and he became quite adventuresome while living in Colorado and later in California.

That spring, before he left Cleveland for the milder winters and less humid summers of Denver, he heard the evangelist Dwight L. Moody, himself about to leave Chicago to speak in England at the invitation of churches there. Moody explained his call, noting, "I like to think big things for God! Do you? . . . The reason I like to think big things for God is that He deserves it. Now whether it's evangelism, or your work, or your money, whatever it is, you ought to think of big ways you can be used for God."

Moody recalled the words of Henry Varley, whom he had met in Ireland: "The world has yet to see what God can do with and for and through and in a man who is fully and wholly consecrated to Him." Then Moody said of Varley's statement, "That was like the Word of God to my soul. Those words pierced my heart. Listen! . . . 'A man.' And Varley meant any man! He didn't say he had to be educated."[2]

Listening to Moody's powerful words, Crowell heard God's call as well. He had left school early because of his health, and now he wondered about his future education. When the meeting was over, Crowell walked along the shore of Lake Erie, lost in thought. Finally he sat down on a large rock, still moved by Moody's words.

"God, there is no mistaking that these have been Your words to me. I can see that You can use me even if I must leave school. Mr. Moody said that I don't have to be an educated man, or brilliant, or anything. Just a man. Lord, by Your grace and with the help of the Holy Spirit, I'll be that man."[3]

Knowing he could never be a preacher, Crowell thought further and concluded: *Maybe I can make money and help support men like D. L. Moody.*

Eventually Henry Crowell went on to create the company we know as Quaker Oats, now headquartered in Chicago. Crowell embraced three core philosophies about stewardship. First, he was a steward of his finances and a most generous man. Second, he believed in stewardship of time. A man of influence places great value on time. Henry used his to help others.

Finally, Crowell was a steward of his *social capital*. He believed God had blessed him with a position of influence, and he chose to use that social capital to help change the city of Chicago. A man like Crowell can do remarkable things to change a culture if he has a heart to serve others.

A useless life is an early death.
■ Goethe

For by him all things were created: things in heaven and on earth, visible and invisible, whether thrones or powers or rulers or authorities; all things were created by him and for him.
■ Colossians 1:16

Jimmy Carter is a living example of this passion for purpose. Although I have strong disagreements with some of President Carter's views, I greatly respect this man as a human being. Carter served as president after becoming the governor of Georgia. He graduated from the U.S. Naval Academy. Perhaps that is where he learned to embrace some of his life values.

Carter faced some very difficult challenges while our president, as all presidents must. People remember the Iranian hostage crisis and the gasoline shortages in particular. But look at Jimmy Carter's life today. What life contribution is he making after holding the most powerful position in the world?

This former president started the Carter Center in Atlanta, a nonpartisan, nonprofit center that addresses national and international issues of public policy. Once a week Jimmy Carter becomes the most famous Sunday school teacher in America . . . in Plains, Georgia. Once a year Jimmy Carter and his wife, Rosalyn, spend a week with Habitat for Humanity, something they have enjoyed doing for twenty-plus years. The former first couple help build homes for those in need. Carter continues to act as a neutral observer at elections in Africa and the Middle East and has earned the respect of the international community.

President Carter's ongoing commitment is proof of his belief in servant leadership. Jimmy Carter is concerned about his fellow man and wants his life to reflect the spirit of a cause greater than himself.

Answers to Your Purpose Questions

If you are now (or once again) looking for an answer to your purpose questions, don't be surprised. This is the great internal challenge. Of course, other people can offer perspective, but don't look for them to resolve your search. Answers are found between you and Someone greater than yourself. Seek God's direction and His peace as you seek His purposes for you.

A man's purpose is fulfilled when he finds something bigger and better than himself to which to offer up his life. May God bless you as you continue to pursue your passion of purpose.

Takeaways

Each chapter will include specific ideas to help you apply the concepts presented. I call them "takeaways." As you consider the impact of purpose in your life, here are some key points to take away:

- *If you're on the right kind of life quest and if you want to avoid burnout, ambition must be tempered by self-control.* It isn't somebody else's job to hold your ambition in check.

■ *If you want a heritage worth remembering, always connect honor with duty.* It isn't enough to do the duty. Honor must go alongside with duty if you're going to be a man of great purpose.

■ *If you want to satisfy your calling, follow the desires of your heart as God gives opportunity and directs your spirit.* The Holy Spirit is the Person of God who gives you internal guidance. The closer you draw to God, the closer He gets to you through the Holy Spirit. That's how you validate your ambitions.

■ *In order to live with purpose, you must determine a cause worth pursuing.* Don't expect a burning bush to resolve the issue for you. It is something you seek out as part of your life journey.

Principles . . . of Passion

For each session, I have also prepared a set of guiding principles. These make good discussion topics for a small group or items to pray about in your life. As you think about your own passion for purpose, here are some principles upon which to reflect.

1. *A man of purpose recognizes the importance of the question, "Why am I here?"* Perhaps today is the day that you really started thinking about that question. Many men drift through life and leave this nagging issue unattended in their soul. Do you believe God has uniquely equipped you and that there is a purpose you are to fulfill? Or are you just going through the motions?

2. *A man of purpose can affirm, "I have responded to my calling."* I have met many men who wonder if they should quit a job and enter into ministry or change careers. How does a man know the answer to this? One way is to remove the idea that he cannot serve God in his current job. He may be exactly God's

man for that role. Again, motivation is the key. Are you living to serve others? And are you using your gifts? Unless you hear a clarion call in your soul to move, don't.

3. *A man of purpose determines priorities in his life and lives by them.* My good friend and mentor Glenn Murray was the first man to walk me through the matter of priorities. I was at a point in my life when I felt overcommitted.

Glenn asked if I could identify my priorities, and I told him, "Well, God is my priority, and my wife is next, then my kids, and my job." He suggested I write these out *along with a paragraph defining their importance.* That exercise made me recognize that saying them was one thing, but living them was quite another.

Next, Glenn had me keep a weekly record of where my time was spent. I was about halfway through the week and realized that my schedule did not match my stated priorities. Over the next several days, I found myself canceling events and rearranging my life to get back in balance. This is not a once-in-a-lifetime exercise. It needs to be repeated and shared with family members (who will check you on it) on a regular basis.

Notes

1. Charles Haddon Spurgeon, *Morning and Evening* (Grand Rapids: Christian Classics, n.d.), Evening, June 27.

2. Joe Musser, *Cereal Tycoon* (Chicago: Moody, 1997), 37–38.

3. Ibid., 39.

Insights on Purpose
. . . with Bob Lepine

During the sixth grade, I decided I wanted to be a lawyer because I watched Perry Mason on television. That actually stuck with me all through college—I planned to go to law school.

I took a summer job at a radio station. They came to me halfway through the summer and said, "Why don't you just keep doing radio? You can go to law school later if you want." And I remember a day when I went out to lunch and prayed, "Lord, what should I do? Should I go to law school, or should I stay in radio?"

I really wrestled with this, and I was not getting any sense of direction from the Lord . . . until the end of the week when I had to make a decision. When I prayed about it that day, it was like the Lord said, "You know what, it doesn't really matter to Me. You can go to law school; you can do radio. Because My ultimate purpose for your life is not foundationally about what you do in a vocation. It's about who you are for Me. And I can accomplish that whether you're a lawyer or whether you're a broadcaster."

I think it's very important for men to connect meaning to their work in life. We talk about "what I do for a living" or about "my occupation." But the word *vocation* really means your calling. I think it's important for us not just to have a job we occupy, but to really seek a calling—something we can do that has nobility and purpose, that serves others, and that honors God.

When we see that our work really does have a sense of nobility and divine purpose, it elevates everything. Just before the Protestant Reformation, men viewed the priestly work as the only godly work. If you were a blacksmith or if you were a cobbler or if you were involved in some trade, you weren't doing God's work. But during the Reformation, we began to see that everything we do, every action we take, can be done to the glory of God. They recognized the truth of 1 Corinthians 10, "Whether you eat or drink or whatever you do, do it all for the glory of God" (verse 31).

Our work is not just the nine-to-five grind that so many of us think of it as. When we see that through our work we can reflect the glory of God, create things that reflect God's glory, and help others, we can get out of bed with a different attitude in the mornings.

If you hear yourself saying about your job, *Well, this isn't going anywhere*, ask yourself why. God has created each of us with unique talents, gifts, and abilities. When we say a job isn't going anywhere, perhaps the job is not bringing out the best of who God made you to be. If that's the case, then maybe you ought to be looking for other work. It may also be that the company that you're involved with isn't really focused and doesn't really have a direction and so you're not really serving others the way you ought to be. If that's the case, maybe you need to be looking around and seeing what God might have.

However, here's a caution: Make sure that you're not expecting more from your job than God intends for you to expect.

Our job is not designed to meet all of our emotional needs for us. And if you're in a job and you're frustrated and say, "I'm just not sure that this is the right job for me," you need to pray hard about that. You need to get some outside counsel. You may be expecting more from a job and from a vocation than God intends for there to be.

On the other hand, if you've found one great job, great! But be careful not to have "an affair" with your work. I've met men who were deriving more sense of meaning and satisfaction from a job than they ought to. We can get seduced by our work. And it's easy to see how it happens. Around the office, people are patting you on the back and saying, "Good job, way to go. That proposal was outstanding! You made that sale! Way to go!" And you feed off that.

Be careful. You may go home and your wife says, "How come you can't take care of this?" and the kids say, "Why can't I get shoes like this?" and you think, *Man, I want to go back to work where they like me, where they admire me, where they respect me.*

Remember, your job is not designed to meet your emotional needs. What will truly matter in the later years are those relationships with your wife, with your family, with your friends. That's where you and I need to be cultivating and working.

Bob Lepine is cohost with Dennis Rainey of the popular radio program Family Life Today. *He speaks at marriage and family seminars around the country.*

*When you come to a fork
in the road, take it.*

—Yogi Berra

◼

*Be strong and courageous.
Do not be afraid or terrified
because of them, for the LORD your
God goes with you; he will never
leave you nor forsake you.*

—Deuteronomy 31:6

2 The Passion for Adventure

It was dawn in Chicago, and our radio station was following a news story emerging under the August morning sun. Media members were already on the scene at the famous Sears Tower. Their interest was piqued by man who was scaling this 110-story, 1,454-foot building—then the world's second largest.

It was the French Spider-Man—Alain Robert. And he made it!

It was not Alain's first attempt at such a daredevil feat. He had previously climbed the Empire State Building and the Eiffel Tower. When he made it to the top, he was greeted by Sears Tower workers . . . and the Chicago police. They don't take kindly to such spectacles. At a minimum, it is trespassing.

Since the Sears Tower is close to the financial district of Chicago, Robert had his share of onlookers. One of them, a futures broker named Holly Liss, commented, "I think it's great!" But, of course! A futures broker knows a fair amount about risky ventures.

Robert had a safety harness on him during the climb, but let's be honest. What kind of man would do such a crazy stunt? That's easy.

Lots of men (and women) are ready to engage in similar feats of daring on a regular basis.

Thrill Seekers

Today, for example, we have "extreme sports." There is even a television channel dedicated to these thrill seekers. And the varieties of ways to almost kill yourself seem endless: bungee jumping, kite surfing, mountain biking, rock climbing, and snowboarding are only a few. In fact, one extreme sport is dedicated to "buildering"—yes, it is the skill of climbing structures!

Many find a great sense of accomplishment in tackling danger. As they conquer their fears, they feel both exhilaration and confidence. They feel they are in a fraternity, knowing they have advanced beyond what most men are willing to face.

Human history is full of people who love to live on the edge. In fact, that must have been wired into our early explorers. Willing to take on life-and-death adventures, men were willing to take to the high seas . . . or cross over thousands of miles of wilderness to see what lies ahead.

Or fly the first supersonic plane. Having met Chuck Yeager, I recall the admiration I felt for this test pilot who cast his fate to the wind for a place in human history—becoming the first man to break the sound barrier. Five years after that feat he flew a newer test plane at more than twice the speed of sound—1,650 mph.

But wait! Is adventure-seeking limited to only those acts of physical danger? Or are there other perilous and risky ways to find those same thrills satisfied? Certainly. People who risk their fortunes or their success on a deal that could cause them to lose it all are men of steel of a different breed.

Men were designed with a spirit of adventure. Of the passions we own, this one usually has the most fun attached. Something about risk and the unknown attracts most men. And when held in balance by our other responsibilities, adventure is what makes our lives exciting!

Great Adventure #1

One of my most significant life adventures started back in 1984. I had worked in radio for several years in programming and sales management. During this time, I had established some strong business relationships and I decided that it was time for me to try my hand at starting a business. As every entrepreneur knows, excitement percolates when you are ready to launch your new enterprise. Well . . . it is often a combination of healthy *fear* and excitement. There is no shortage of a sense of adventure!

My venture was going to specialize in video production. We were living in Grass Valley, California (outside Sacramento), an area known for innovation and risk taking. This was home to the Grass Valley Group. These folks designed sophisticated video switchers and were on the cutting edge of emerging technologies. I was following these trends in video technology and believed there was a growing demand for relatively low-cost video production.

Admittedly, I wasn't a video expert myself. I had more of a sales and marketing background and knew that marketing skills would be critical to the success of a company. The strategy was to develop a prototype video production business and then franchise it. It wasn't difficult to find freelance camera and production people to do the actual work.

I found a good attorney, formed a Sub S corporation, and found thirty-five seed investors who believed in me . . . and my business plan. After six months I had raised about half the amount of capital for which my business plan called. When the existing investors approved my revised sales plan, I set sail into the seas of business adventure. Make that the rough seas of business adventure.

Like all start-ups, this one had its own struggles. A little less than two years later, I woke up in the middle of the night in a cold sweat. I realized the stark truth: The company I had created was not going to make it. I knew that I would have to call my investors together—people who invested in me as much as my idea—and tell them the news. This was agonizing because these were people who trusted me and believed that I had the vision, the strength, and the wisdom to make this work. Dare I say it? I was going to have to admit failure.

It wasn't that this business wasn't producing. In the first year and a half of operations I was within 5 percent of my projections for both revenue and expense. But we ran out of money . . . right on schedule. Employees were going to lose their jobs. All that sweat equity was going to be lost as well. And what about my reputation?

I was in my midthirties, and I really felt that I had captured an idea that would work. I had tried my best. It was difficult to admit defeat. However, what makes any adventure an adrenaline builder is *the possibility that you might lose.*

Life is either a daring
adventure or nothing.
■ Helen Keller

It is not good to have zeal without knowledge,
nor to be hasty and miss the way.
■ Proverbs 19:2

There was much to be learned from this experience. Even today, I find myself relying on principles that developed from my business failure. That is another piece in the pursuit of adventure: learning what to avoid and what to do better the next time.

My wife, Rhonda, was grateful that I was a man of vision and that I dreamed of big things. She liked the idea that if things would have worked we could have had a nicer nest and financial security.

However, the risk thing bothered her. Early on, she opposed the risks that would face us from my entrepreneurial longings. Many women are uncomfortable with taking chances. Security is a very important issue for them. Obviously, when the venture went south and we had to live without income for a period of time, it created new challenges in our relationship. (That may be an understatement.) God's grace saw us through this experience and our marriage commitment made the difference.

Great Adventure #2

A second adventure of mine occurred in 1994. A Bible distribution ministry was putting together a team of radio broadcasters to travel to the Far East. Our mission was to meet with Christians in a certain country, some of whom had been persecuted for their faith. We were also to bring along a few Bibles to share with these young believers. We were warned that these Bibles could be confiscated and that we could be detained.

I received a very official looking document titled, "Briefing Paper for Mark Elfstrand." The paper described the various activities in which we would engage during our visit. But it also laid out some realistic risks. In several Far Eastern countries, religious tolerance is a mixed bag. Many followers of Christ do not believe they can meet openly as they fear governmental reprisal. A degree of religious freedom exists, but it varies from country to country and province to province.

I was being advised that some of our private meetings could pose risks. We could be seen as undermining government efforts to monitor religion. Of course, the people we met with faced a greater risk. But we were reminded that government controls were in place and we might be vulnerable to searches or some form of interrogation.

I took this briefing paper home and called a family meeting to share with them this opportunity. My oldest son, Marshall, then age sixteen, listened as I read of the stated risks and dangers that might accompany our trip. We were even told that our personal safety could not be guaranteed.

After I finished reading, I turned to my family and asked, "Well, what do you think? Should I go???"

Without a moment of hesitation, Marshall said, "I'll go!" The very idea that we could do something that would encourage other Christians in a faraway place thrilled his soul. And *his* response thrilled me.

The trip went very well. And I made several subsequent trips to several other countries for the same purpose over the next few years. On one of those trips, in a country I shall not name, our group was followed by the secret police. One particular evening, a group of us went out for dinner and noticed we were being "tailed." After dinner, we split up in two taxis, leaving our police escort confused over which group to follow.

To this point, we had chosen not to call home from our hotel lest our calls be monitored. The group in my taxi determined we were not being followed and we took the opportunity to stop and place a call to our families by using a public phone and our calling cards. Needless to say, my wife was *not* impressed with my sense of adventure, tricking a security detail in a foreign country. She did not consider it one of my shining moments. But it was a great adventure!

Components of Adventure

Ten great passions define men, and one of them is unquestionably the passion for adventure. Men love excitement, challenges, and competition. Yet this passion, like the other nine, can get out of control. The objective is for us to do a gut check on our own lives. We want to be men who live in balance.

The Unknown

Like the passion of purpose, this passion of adventure has four components, or aspects. The first is dealing with *the unknown*—that which arouses a man's curiosity. This curiosity begins for us as little boys. It shows up when our parents can't seem to find us as we are out conquering the mysteries of life. We are out seeking adventure!

Of course, sometimes as little guys we got lost—like in a department store! We might have been a bit terrified by this but not as terrified as our parents. However, getting lost does *not* deter a boy from further adventures. We are built for it.

The Thrill

Adventure also includes *the thrill*—that which exhilarates the human spirit. One of the most thrilling and stupid things I did in high school was to go "drag racing" with one of my friends. My dad had a Ford with a 390-cubic-inch engine. My buddy had a Chevrolet with a 350 cube. He thought his 350 could beat my 390, so we went outside of town to prove ourselves and our machines.

We found a starting point that would take us a half mile or so— over a couple of hills. I got in the left lane, he was in the right. Our speed got up to 110 or 115 miles an hour going up and down hills, *over which we could not see.* It was exhilarating, though not very bright. A man—and a teenage guy—thrive on thrill.

Risk

The third aspect of adventure is *risk*. Risk is that which tests a man under pressure. Risk is where we put it all on the line. Risk comes with various levels; the higher the stakes, the greater the drama. Men who take great personal risks are often admired for their courage and the ability "not to sweat."

Living Dangerously

The fourth aspect is *living dangerously*. It is the kind of adventure that compels a man to walk on the edge. Many extreme sports today seem to fit this category. The downside of this is reckless living, where a man puts himself and others in harm's way.

Life as Risky Business

Recapping, when we pursue the unknown, we have the urge to explore, the urge to experience, and ultimately the urge to conquer. When we seek out thrills, that which exhilarates the human spirit, we find that these thrills are a test of our courage. It is at this point in life that men begin to shape what kind of adventurer they will be. While it is true that some men overcome fears later in life and become more adventuresome, early failures often seem to put a cap on a man's spirit.

In taking what are perceived as "chances"—that which tests a man under pressure—we learn that life is risky business. The astute man knows that the future is truly unpredictable. We don't know what awaits us when we leave for work each morning. Despite living with the unknown, the adventurer is not troubled by that. He accepts it.

If a man is a healthy adventurer, he knows the difference between good risks and bad risks. He prefers what we call calculated risks. We take thirty-year mortgages because we believe our investment will grow over time as will our income to pay for that home. Buying a home is risky, but it is a calculated risk. Bad risks are those where the odds grow increasingly against us. Anyone who has studied the impact of gambling understands this. The success of any casino rests on people taking foolish risks. The odds are always stacked against them. Yet there are many men willing to put down their weekly earnings in hopes of achieving ill-gotten gain.

Be careful of that final component, living dangerously. It tempts many men to walk on the edge. Men who like to walk on the edge will even choose a line of work that enables them to do that. Window washers and high-rise construction workers who glide along beams sixty stories above the ground come to mind. Policemen, firemen, and undercover agents fit the bill, as do circus performers.

But for some men, living dangerously reveals a bent to prove something. This is where a man's desire for adventure gets out of balance.

If you're willing to take on dangerous activity in order to prove something, you are not a healthy adventurer.

The Adventure Continuum

Clearly, balance is the key on the adventure continuum. We know that man is wired with a passion for adventure and we know it's in us from our earliest age. However, as a man ages (sorry, we all "age" after we turn twenty-one), he can move out of balance. Often he loses his sense of adventure or no longer follows his dream.

On the left side of the continuum you will find the man who we might well refer to as *the ultraconservative*. He is the man who always looks for the safe bet; he will not challenge the system. He avoids risks, and he fears confrontation, especially with people in charge. This man has a very small comfort zone and doesn't want to move out of it. New situations are to be avoided and particularly if there is any risk of embarrassment or failure at any level.

Another side effect of the ultraconservative's life is his attitude toward his work. Very often, he lacks passion for excellence. Again, his effort might not get rewarded; it might even be rejected. So why try? The biblical word for this is *sloth*. Eventually, this is the man who finds little satisfaction in life because he has lost any sense of adventure.

On the other end of the spectrum is *the thrill seeker*. This man is constantly looking for the next way to get the adrenaline rush. He is prone to be a gambler. He is willing to put it all on the table, or in the game of life. On the highway he seems to drive as a possessed man.

In the office he is always willing to take the chance road, whatever that may be. He lives for someone to say . . . "Dare me."

In accounting practices, he will always play the gray areas. In business, he will be aggressively careless. His home life can become boring if there is not enough stimulation, so he will find outside activities to pursue to satisfy this urge for thrills.

Every man fits somewhere on the continuum of adventure. Where are you? Our objective is to be men who are centered and balanced.

If you are living on the cautionary left side of the continuum, you are missing a part of God's design of manhood. Remember, without risk of peril or danger, great expeditions would never have been led. Great evangelistic moves would have been abandoned, great inventions would not exist, and medical breakthroughs would be virtually impossible. And God cannot show His power and involvement if we do not take those first steps away from our cozy comfort zones.

A man leaning too much on the security side needs to proactively move to the right. How does he do that? He must give careful thought to what constitutes risk for him—and take a risk at times. It might be a physical adventure, becoming transparent in a relationship, making a career move, or setting new goals for his life that require him to step out in faith. And that is a vital part of his return to adventure—realizing God is in control and exercising faith that God will bring about good as manhood is embraced. Of course, any significant life change should be made with counsel and certainly with support from spouse and family.

Conversely, if you are living at the far right in the continuum, you are at risk of foolishness. You may well irritate people with unnecessary gamesmanship. People will consider you a loose cannon, not to be trusted. You can be considered careless and way too aggressive. In business, you can put your team and their well-being in jeopardy.

Your family can wind up suffering. A thrill seeker will constantly look for the next "high" to be gained to support his risk habit. You will not be a good role model for your children.

This man must shift to the left. He must examine himself and be honest about his love for the thrill. If he has habits of gambling, or evidence of risky adventures or investments, he needs to consider restraint. Getting input from friends and family who can give an honest assessment of your heart for risk will help. Most men know if they are out of balance.

High-risk takers might also consider the spiritual dynamic involved. Faith to move forward and trust in God is one thing. But taking unnecessary risks can be interpreted as testing God. This is never a good idea. While you might succeed occasionally, there are usually dire consequences for the man who constantly walks on the edge.

The balanced adventurer realizes that risks are always present, but he seeks to downsize those risks by proper preparation and weighing the consequences. He seeks wisdom through divine intervention and by godly counsel of other men. The Bible teaches us to be men who employ wisdom, and we must seek that wisdom when it comes to our adventures.

Manhood Models

Neil Armstrong is one of many explorers whose spirit for adventure could not be shaken. At age nine, he was an aircraft nut who loved all kinds of planes. When he joined the elite group of young American astronauts in 1962, he did so almost reluctantly. He preferred the experience of flying where he was in control. He loved flying fast airplanes and even experimental kinds of aircrafts.

Neil Armstrong grew up in middle America (Wapakoneta, Ohio) during the Depression. By the time he was fourteen, he had passed through an extensive model airplane–building stage, and that year he was up in a real airplane learning how to fly thanks to a friend who owned a flying school. By his sixteenth birthday, he had his pilot's license—Neil Armstrong could fly before he could drive.

Armstrong once said the single thing that makes any man happiest is the realization that he has worked up to the limits of his ability, to his own capacity. "It's all the better," he said, "if this work has contributed to knowledge or toward moving the human race a little farther forward."

Neil joined the U.S. Navy after attending Purdue University. He was assigned to the carrier USS *Essex* after receiving naval flight training. Armstrong once coaxed a badly crippled jet back to the deck of the *Essex*. At another point, during the Korean War, he was shot down behind enemy lines and rescued the next day. Armstrong survived near-miss experiences in experimental aircraft.

Two of his most hair-raising adventures were a middle-of-the-night fire in his Texas home and the problem-plagued flight on *Gemini 8*. That was the only manned space flight to date that had to be brought home early because of the problems. As command pilot on the *Gemini* mission, he performed the first docking of two vehicles in space.

Of course, Armstrong is best known as commander of the *Apollo 11* mission, when he became the first astronaut to land a spacecraft on the moon—and then the first man to step on the moon's surface.

Although he was willing to take great risk to travel all the way to the moon, Armstrong says he did so with calculated success behind him: "I have been in relatively high-risk businesses all of my adult life. I have confidence in the equipment, the planning, the training, and I suspect that on a risk/gain ratio, space missions would compare very, very favorably with those to whom I've been accustomed these past twenty years."

The *apostle Paul* remains a great manhood model for adventure! The account of his life and adventures are chronicled in the book of Acts in the Bible, particularly the last few chapters of that book. His missionary journeys, his shipwrecks, his meeting with kings, and seeing the miracles of God all create an enormous adventure! Read his accounts and you will learn that when God calls a man to serve, an exciting adventure awaits.

Paul had something that guided and encouraged him in a deeper way: the absolute assurance that his earthly life was only a prelude to a greater event to come. In later biblical writings, Paul told fellow believers in Christ that he could not determine whether it was better to live or die . . . because of the great reward that awaited him. The true adventurer who knows God is able to grasp that kind of faith. Once it sinks in—the permanence of our heavenly home—we can approach risks and dangers with great confidence and hope.

Overcoming the Fear

Some men fear the big adventures so much they avoid the small ones. But that's all wrong; start with the small ones, and those will prepare you for the big ones.

Many years ago, I started experiencing panic attacks. The first one was at the age of nineteen. And I remember distinctly where I was when it happened—at the top of the Space Needle. I had been up in the Space Needle, Seattle's landmark observation tower and restaurant, several times previously. However, on this occasion, I felt like I had an urge to climb over the glass barrier and jump. I was not at all suicidal, so having this thought blew me out of the proverbial Puget Sound water. The distance from top to bottom is about six hundred feet.

Sheer, literal terror came over me and I wanted to sit down right on the spot and hold on to something. I almost asked for someone to restrain me because I had these two conflicting things going on in my mind: "I don't want to do this, so why am I feeling this urge?" That created in me a pretty serious fear of heights. I never wanted to go up in buildings that were extremely tall, and especially those elevators that go from zero to the top floor with no stops in between.

Over time, that fear began to manifest itself in other ways. For example, I didn't like long bridges. *I didn't want to be in any situation where I wasn't in control.* My fears moved next to airplanes. Once I got in the airplane and they shut the door, and we were "locked in" and I knew I couldn't get out for a couple of hours, there was a feeling of panic. Usually for a guy, takeoffs are the most exciting part of the flight. For me, it became the most terrifying.

> *It is only in adventure that some people succeed in knowing themselves—in finding themselves.*
> ■ *André Gide*
>
> *When I called, you answered me; you made me bold and stouthearted.*
> ■ *Psalm 138:3*

Today, I can cross oceans on airplanes. I can go over long bridges (although the Mackinac Island bridge in upper Michigan still might test me a bit . . . as may those very long bridges connecting the Florida Keys). The Lord has worked in my life to remove almost any trace of a panic attack. Occasionally I have the sensations of one coming on, but I have been spared.

My healing in this area began with a series of small steps. For some men, making adventurous moves may require the same process. If panic sets in when you consider risk taking, take small risks first and build up.

Fear is what usually keeps a man from being adventurous. Fear can often be defeated incrementally. Maybe that is why it is said you have to "work *up* your courage"!

Takeaways

There are some key concepts we can apply as we seek to properly use our passion for adventure. Here are a few:

- *As a man on the right kind of quest for adventure, you will realize that if you are bored or boring, it is because you lack adventure in your life.* And there is really only one person who can solve that: *you!* There are many resources for men who want to take on a new adventure. Look for some of those with a friend.

- *If you seek adventure, you must cope with risk and the unknown.* It is inherent in the adventure mind-set. In fact, it is what builds excitement into the equation. Like the first ride on a new roller coaster or theme park experience, the unknown and the outcomes of that experience give you something to talk about.

- *You will not experience the depth of your manhood until you experiment with adventure.* For some men, displaying a test of courage is needed. And it usually happens in the progression of risk-taking success. For another man, it might be trial by fire. But if you want to experience life more deeply as a man, you must widen your world of adventure.

- *Your adventure need not be life threatening to be life changing.* There are many fears and frustrations that hold men back. Some of those are physical, some of those are emotional, some of those are mental. Overcoming past fears (and present ones as well) may require bold effort to go where you have not gone before. Physical danger need not be present to get you past your previous barriers in life.

- *To make the adventure leap, you must be willing to risk exposing a weakness.* John Eldredge, whose insights conclude this chapter, writes a fair amount about a particular fear that men share: the fear of being discovered. He found that to be true in his own life—that he was simply pretending to be somebody who he was not. The reason that we encourage men to be a part of small groups—in or outside of the church—is to help them develop a means of intimacy, to reveal themselves. (For more on developing intimacy, read chapter 9.)

Principles . . . of Adventure

As you consider your life as a man and adventurer, consider these principles:

1. *A man of adventure understands that God expects him to live with the unknown and yet have a deep sense of confidence.* The Lord is observing us. He is observing you in your development as a man. Our God finds special kingdom purposes for men who are willing to entrust their lives wholly and fully to Him. God will give you all the adventure you can handle if your trust is in Him.

2. *A man of adventure chooses wisdom over foolishness in making decisions.* I don't know of any man who would not admit to making some bad decisions in life. While not prone to admit we are wrong, men do recognize bad judgment when it occurs. But the poor adventurer continues to make foolish decisions. And he often refuses counsel. A wise man learns from his mistakes and uses the learning of others to avoid future mistakes.

3. *A man of adventure lives with risk but recognizes that outcomes are not under his control.* As I shared with you my personal story about panic attacks, perhaps you picked up that I was dealing with the issue of control. I wanted to be in control over my circumstances. An unstable environment and a lack of perceived safety in that situation made me very uncomfortable. The most troubling aspect of these attacks was that I could not control my own racing heart.

Control is a big issue for men. We like to control our surroundings and our circumstances. The man of adventure lives with risk, realizing that outcomes are not under his control. My healing process in dealing with panic included the recognition that it was my response that needed to change, not the circumstances.

Insights on Adventure
. . . *with John Eldredge*

I believe the desire for adventure is wired into the heart of every man. Now, not every man wants to go jump off cliffs or hang glide or hunt alligators in the Amazon. That's not what I mean by adventure. But every man needs a sense of *risk* in his life. Guys who e-trade stocks? That's adventure. Guys who are on the cutting edge of research science? That's adventure. These men are looking for discovery; they're looking for breakthrough.

That longing for adventure goes back to the time when guys were little boys. What do little boys love to do? They love to explore, they love to overcome challenges, and they want to simply go! Boys don't just want to ride their bikes. They want to ride their bikes with no hands! They want to jump them off the curb. They want to see who can go fastest down the hill. There really is something in every man that was wired for adventure from boyhood.

I think that sense of adventure gets tamed out of us. We also get frightened. Somewhere along the way, a man loses that confidence, that recklessness or fearlessness he had as a boy. Somewhere along the story of his life, a doubt comes in. And a doubt goes like this: "No you don't. You don't have what it takes. You can't come through. You can't pull this off. So just put your nose to the horse in front of you and get in line and just become a gelding. Tie your reins up there at the corporate corral and give up any sense of risk."

I remember waking up one morning to realize that I hated my life. I'm wearing a suit and tie and I'm working in politics. And I don't like suits and ties and I don't like politics. I realized that somewhere along the way I had abandoned my dreams and my desires as a man.

To be a true man doesn't mean you have to go jump out of an airplane. To be a true man, you must live with courage and you must accept the risks that God is asking you to walk into.

Such risks may express themselves in lots of different ways, depending on the way a particular man is wired. For one man, the biggest risk in his life is writing that book he always wanted to write. For another man, it is taking a promotion which will put him into a leadership position that he doesn't know he can fulfill. For another man, the biggest risk of his life is actually selling his business and spending more time with his kids. The point is . . . courage.

For those who seek courage, God is there. He takes a man and tells him *who he is*. He gives him his *genuine identity*. When Jesus comes out of the Jordan River as He is baptized, the Father speaks and says, "I am so proud of You. I couldn't be more pleased with You." That's what every man longs to hear from his father. We may not be able to get that from our fathers now, and so we must turn to God.

When Jesus announces His ministry in Luke 4, He offers to heal the brokenhearted and set the captive free (Isaiah 61:1). Jesus says, "I really have come not *just* to forgive you, I want to give you back your heart. I want to *heal you*." It's a message of God wanting to restore us as men. Really restore us.

But that can only take place if you will take that fear, that uncertainty—and especially that woundedness—to Him and let God father you.

John Eldredge is the author of several best-selling books, including The Sacred Romance *and* Wild at Heart. *He loves to do rock climbing, kayaking, and mountain biking.*

Our scientific power has outrun our spiritual power. We have guided missiles and misguided men.

—Martin Luther King Jr.

■

Then Jesus came to them and said, "All authority in heaven and on earth has been given to me."

—Matthew 28:18

3 The Passion for Power

Hollywood does a masterful job of creating characters we want to see destroyed. Clint Eastwood as Dirty Harry chased a serial killer who buried a girl alive. And eventually Harry took "justice" into his own hands. Mel Gibson as patriot Benjamin Martin, a peaceful farmer, led a colonial militia in an uprising after a sadistic British officer murdered his son. As a father of two sons, I remember the anger and desire to see retaliation against this British officer, as I watched the movie *The Patriot*.

These are the classic stories of good guys—as we see them—taking on (and often taking out) the bad guys.

What is it about those evil characters that causes us to feel powerful emotions such as anger and even hatred? I believe it is watching power that is out of control. When we see an abuse of power that hurts and sometimes devastates others, most of us feel the victim's pain. And we want what we think they want: revenge!

I have major memories of being intimidated by power during the eighth grade. Those years of junior high can be brutal for young guys. Boys who have "power issues" start revealing those tendencies early.

Bullies and Power

One kid in particular manifested the true "bully" personality. I was a new kid in the school and for some reason he made me his target. He would come to me periodically and ask to borrow a couple bucks. Since I worked for my dad at the restaurant he managed, I usually did have some cash on me. Several times I gave him a "loan." After several of these loans, it became clear he did not plan to repay me for my kindness. And so on one occasion during gym class, he came to me for more money.

He approached as the guys were changing clothes at their lockers. The bully boy made his request and I turned him down, explaining he owed me quite a bit of money. He responded by grabbing me by my T-shirt and jamming me against the locker. Then he removed my pants from my locker, reached in and took several bills. Finally he threw my pants back in my locker and walked off. For an eighth-grader, this was sheer humiliation.

I had a similar experience about a year later, but in a different school. We had recently moved back to Minnesota from Illinois. It was now my freshman year and by then I was wearing glasses. One day another of these young renegades decided to come up behind me, remove my glasses, and challenge me to "find him"—as if I could not see without my glasses.

I stood there calmly and said, "Come on, Gerry—just give 'em back."

He wouldn't. Finally he just tossed them on the floor toward me while making some rude comment. He had a couple of his buddies with him; they all left, laughing at me.

While I can't remember a lot of my classmates from junior high—in fact very few of them—I easily remember the names of those two boys. Those were painful experiences for a junior high kid. There are some who will read these accounts and know exactly how I felt. There will be some others who see in these stories their own life—as a bully!

As an adult, I came to understand that those kinds of incidents were about power. The exercise of that power was to intimidate. The test of that power was to find victims. The success of that power was to exploit weakness.

The frightening thing we learn about those displays of power is that perpetrators often grow up to live as adults trying to live by the same rules. And without a taming influence in their lives, this lust for power can be a devastating and uncontrollable weakness.

But you don't have to be a bully to learn to abuse power—it can become a controlling weakness in our lives. That is what we will look at in this chapter: how to get the passion for power under control.

Physical Strength and Power

I'm a big Dave Barry fan. In one his columns, Barry writes:

> I started lifting weights but not for the reason you think. You think I want to look cut and ripped and have bulging muscles like the ones on male underwear models, who for some reason are always shown posing outdoors. . . .
>
> You think I want to have muscles like that so women will look at me and think, "Wow, I would like to see his syndicated column." But you're wrong. I'm lifting weights for sensible medical reasons. . . . I found out from the internet when you get to be my age—old—you lose bone density and muscle mass. This alarmed me because I never had any muscle mass to begin with.
>
> It was a difficult time for me but my mom one day, bless her heart, had a talk with me. She told me that girls were not only interested in looks, but the qualities that really mattered were brains and a sense of humor. That little talk was long ago, but it taught me an invaluable lesson that I have never forgotten. Moms lie when they have to.[1]

In reality, for about the first fifteen years of life, physical strength *is* the benchmark of personal power among boys. Whether it's arm wrestling, king of the hill, or later those high school sports—physical strength is where the power curve really is. Later, academic and mental strength will become power mechanisms as well. As a sophomore, I joined the high school debate team. That same year my debate team won the district debate championship. Frankly, I enjoyed some of my own moments of intimidation on a different kind of playing field. Simply stated, I found I could abuse power as well. Verbal skills wield another kind of power.

Other Kinds of Power

Mental prowess and verbal skills that translate into political power drive our world. Many business and political leaders may have physical strength, but it is not by the physical side that they are known. Yet they make decisions that affect the lives of billions on our planet.

Among the most dramatic kinds of everyday power we witness in American culture is economic power. You can control corporations, governments, and individuals by holding the power of the dollar in your hand. Wealthy men like Bill Gates and Warren Buffett carry enormous influence—translated as power.

Having rank is another kind of power. There is a reason we call it "climbing the corporate ladder." With the right position you can put people on their backs. For men like Donald Trump, the future of an employee can crash with two words: "You're fired." And here is the oddity. A man like Trump can say that to a physically strong man who was once king of the hill. Maybe he was the most valuable football player in high school. With those two words, he can appear to the world like an unemployed failure.

Yes, there are many kinds of power, and make no mistake about it—men desire it. Some men are consumed by it.

Components of Power

To understand how power works and its limits, let's look at five components of this passion: *strength, intimidation, leadership, control,* and *domination.*

Strength

Strength is the internal and external force needed to accomplish something. Men admire and desire physical strength. One place where this is clearly demonstrated is Olympic competition. Olympic athletes show their strength and endurance. They train tirelessly for years to win the gold, silver, even bronze medals of excellence.

And men love watching contact sports, like football. We enjoy watching football players making the big hits. Some hockey fans love body checks that turn out a guy's lights. Yes, physical strength is impressive to us as men.

Often mental or emotional strength also impresses us. Popular television shows pay contestants ten of thousands of dollars (on one show up to a million dollars) if they can just deal with the mental pressure and answer increasingly tough questions. (As a radio host, I have listened to people being tripped up on easy questions when they melt under the pressure of being live on the radio.)

Strength is any capacity to move things to action. Any step you can take as a man to improve in strength, be it emotional, physical, or mental strength, is a manly thing to pursue. Men admire strength, and it is worthy of our character. Strength is the internal and external force needed to accomplish something.

Intimidation

The second component of power represents one of the uglier sides: *intimidation.* This abuse of power employs force to accomplish selfish ends. When a man faces intimidation and responds by cooperating, it leaves him feeling weak and unmanly. To get a somewhat humorous perspective on this, try watching the movie *The Three Amigos.* Steve Martin, Chevy Chase, and Martin Short play three actors who are heroes of the old West. When they try to stand up to the studio producer and demand more money, they are fired.

Later they receive a telegram from a poor woman in Mexico trying to defend her small village against the dreaded bandit El Guapo and his men. She sees the movies of the three amigos and thinks they will solve her town's problem. She sends a telegram in which her offer is somewhat mistranslated. The amigos jump on the opportunity to help, thinking they are putting on a "show." Instead, they find themselves facing *real* banditos.

As El Guapo and his men come to town to confront the three amigos, there is a skirmish in which Steve Martin is actually hit by a real bullet. The amigos then know they are facing a true criminal and admit they are only actors and beg for forgiveness. They quickly offer to leave town. And in the process, the three men are humiliated.

Although the movie is a humorous look at intimidation, it also has quite a sense of reality. Many are the towns and villages who have their El Guapos . . . power-hungry men who use intimidating tactics to get their way. They use it at home, at the office, and often in running the government. The results are usually devastating.

Intimidation inevitably causes broken relationships. A well-known radio broadcaster in one city was notorious for intimidating coworkers. He would hold weekly staff meetings as the leader of his department. On one occasion, he had a bad headache and was resting at his desk when he fell asleep. The time came for the meeting to start and he was still in his office. Several employees gathered outside but *none* of them would wake this poor chap! They were all too afraid of his response. Now *that* is intimidation . . . and a fractured relationship.

Leadership

A third component of the passion for power has a more positive approach: *leadership*. It may not seem like power and leadership fit together, but they most certainly do. If you have a passion to lead and lead well, it is a healthy, manly quality. Leadership is taking on the role of influence and responsibility over others. Leadership means influence, which is the positive aspect of power.

It is often assumed that leadership roles are granted to those who are most capable. Certainly we know that is not always the case. Would you say the statement *Good followers make good leaders* is true or false? In my experience sometimes it's true, but not always. There are some people that aren't great followers, but they eventually make terrific leaders because they capture the essence of motivating and encouraging others to perform to levels of excellence without damaging their worth along the way.

> *Power is the ability to do good things for others.*
> ■ Brooke Astor
>
> *A wise man has great power, and a man of knowledge increases strength.*
> ■ Proverbs 24:5

In the past decade or so, many books have appeared on servant-leadership. The model for such leadership is Jesus of Nazareth. Jesus never abused His resources of power—and they were unparalleled! The servant-leader keeps power moves in check. He sees that his role is primarily to assist his team in achieving results by enabling them in the best way possible!

Control

Control is a fourth component associated with power. Control is the attempt to manipulate both processes and people. And these efforts may not be overt or forthright. Politics, by legend, is "smoke-filled back room" business. Implied in this is the cutting of deals behind the backs of others. The elements of control are fully engaged as power is brokered by getting control of people and jobs. With its indirect approach, control can be quite different from intimidation.

Control is a huge issue for many men. We want to control outcomes as well as relationships. Until a man learns to give up the need for control, he can do great damage to himself and to others.

Domination

A final component of power is *domination.* Typically this component carries ugly connotations. Domination is the need to overwhelm—even the desire to wipe out. In sports, we often hear the word used. There is the football defense that is "totally dominating." A "dominant player" rules in tennis. While we may admire the skill level of these teams or players, many times we find ourselves cheering for the underdog. Dominance comes from an initially healthy desire to excel at the highest level. Dominance out of control is nothing short of a power-hungry instinct to kill and destroy. God never intended for a man to live in that fashion.

Men who live to dominate can eventually be crushed by their own out-of-balance desires. Whether it is corporate America trying to snuff out the competition, a team that must score one more touchdown to punish the opposition, or a man who must win every argument or contest, the guy who tries to dominate is at risk. He is a man in need of repair.

Power—One of Our Most Dangerous Passions

You will deal with men all your life who struggle with this passion—some without seeing the damage or hurt they inflict. A man's passion for power is among the most dangerous of his passions. Unguided and unrestrained, it becomes a liability that can destroy rather build up.

The first two definitions of *power* in Merriam-Webster's Collegiate Dictionary are worth noting: (1) the ability to act or produce an effect; and (2) possession of control, authority, or influence over others.[2] Being a man of influence is a powerful and wonderful thing. It does not take great physical, mental, or emotional strength. It is a matter of will. You can be highly influential in simple and profound ways. More on that a bit later.

Yet the abuse of power can take place in almost any setting. How about in your home? You will exercise power within your family. You can use intimidation, domination, control tactics . . . or you can employ the servant-leader model that utilizes the ability to influence others.

On the job, you have an opportunity to make a significant difference in the lives of other people as a servant-leader. Or you can dominate, control, or intimidate.

*Excessive power sees
power beyond its power.*
■ Seneca

*This is the word of the LORD to Zerubbabel:
"Not by might nor by power, but by my Spirit,"
says the LORD Almighty."*
■ Zechariah 4:6

Even church leaders can abuse power. Many pastors are control driven. I've seen pastors who are real intimidators.

Here are a few warning signs for the abuse of power. You may have a problem with power if . . .

- You interrupt others and talk over them as if your words were more important. I'm surprised at how often that happens. When someone is in the middle of a sentence, you take over the conversation as though his thoughts were of less significance. That approach reveals a desire to control, to take the power position.

- You want to lead in order to attract the respect and admiration of others. If that is your secret motivation, then you may have a problem with power.

- Your family lives in fear of your next set of demands. No human being feels safe in this environment, and your actions not only cause family life to suffer, but can cause lasting damage to the personalities of those you should love most.

- You make sarcastic and cutting remarks as your way of setting things straight. Although a lesser visible ploy for power, it is nonetheless a means of trying to get the upper hand—a power play.

- You resent authority. This is very common among men and the problem may have some deep underpinnings as to the cause. Let it be said that often men who resent authority use high-control tactics themselves when placed in positions of power.

The Power Continuum

The power continuum is a place to examine yourself for balance. I'm going to use frank terms to describe extremes of this passion.

On the far left is *the wimp*, a weak, cowardly, ineffective person. This is the man who always looks for the safe bet. He won't challenge the system or the people in charge. He has a very tight comfort zone and won't move out of it. If something is new or different or in some way might cause any risk of embarrassment, he avoids it.

When a man feels powerless, he may well succumb to performing with mediocrity or carelessness. Even when we find ourselves battling issues we cannot win, we must not allow our self-pity to give us justification for sloth.

Men of excellence do not wimp out. They realize they are men who are called to stand up and live rightly.

On the other end of our power continuum is *the dictator*. This is the one who rules absolutely and often oppressively. This man is willing to do anything it takes to keep himself in power. Everything is on his terms; he makes the rules. *Flexibility*, *negotiation*, and *compromise* are words missing from his vocabulary. Whether this derives from his conviction of supremacy or just an overworked passion for power, he is definitely out of control on the extreme end of the power continuum.

So where do you fit? You are somewhere on that balance beam. Are you more of the wimp or the dictator? If you are living on the left side of the continuum, you are missing a great part of God's design of manhood. Your leadership skills are lacking and you need to step up to the plate. If you realize you lean more towards the dictator, your life is equally out of balance. You need some self-control, a by-product of having the Spirit of God present in your life.

Our goal is to be men who find the center point of that continuum. What does that center point look like? It has already been described as the servant-leader. Remember that the most powerful man who ever walked the face of the earth had the power at His disposal to call 10,000 angels into action. Jesus, the Creator of the universe—who speaks and the winds and the waves respond—still washed the feet of His closest followers. He walked in humility and even said He came to serve (Mark 10:45). He is the example of power under control. Jesus is the role model and we need hearts and minds like His.

Manhood Models

Here are quick glimpses of two men who learned to balance the passion of power.

The first is *William Wilberforce*, an English citizen and the son of a wealthy merchant. At seventeen, he was sent to St. John's College in Cambridge. He decided on a career of politics and eventually he was elected to the House of Commons.

In 1784, Wilberforce became converted to Christianity. As a result, he became interested in social reform. He was eventually approached by Lady Middleton to use his power as a member of Parliament to bring an end to the slave trade in England. As a member of the evangelical movement, he wanted to respond to this request, and he even said, "I feel the importance of this subject," but then he added, "I think myself unequal to the task allotted to me."

The cynic says, "One man can't do anything." I say, "Only one man can do anything."
■ John W. Gardner

Despite his uncertainty, Wilberforce moved forward and became a key man in the removal of slavery from England. He acted on convictions that resulted from his desire to serve God . . . and be a man of influence for the kingdom.

John Wooden, the superb college basketball coach who led his teams to ten national championships, also learned to use power properly. More than thirty years after his retirement, many admire and follow Wooden's leadership style. John was born in Indiana and went to Purdue University to study civil engineering but became an English major instead—and an outstanding basketball player. He earned a reputation as a fearless guard of dazzling speed. He was an all-American three straight years, led Purdue to a national championship, and later earned a place in college basketball's Hall of Fame. In 1948, he went on to become a coach in basketball. As the coach of the UCLA Bruins, he established an incredible career record of 620 wins and 147 losses, winning 79 percent of his games. Four of his teams were undefeated.

Interestingly, John Wooden might well have had an unguarded strength that at times became an unguarded weakness for him. He used to yell at the refs! Later in his life he admitted that this was a weakness that revealed an area of his life that he needed to exercise more control. But John Wooden is clearly a man who understood the value of good leadership. He used his ability to influence to create teams of greatness.

Your Role

Remember, you likely are a much more powerful person, a person of influence, than you realize. God has designed you and me for leadership. He has given you a role that bears with it the responsibility to act wisely. Use that role to be a person of influence. Used correctly, this power to influence can help change the world.

Takeaways

The man on the right kind of quest for power must know his limitations as well as his call to be a servant-leader. Here are some key points to take away:

■ *A true man must not shrink from the responsibility of power.*
Every man is called to lead in some capacity. You move closer
to the center of the continuum when you recognize that there
is a call on your life to lead. When you understand that a
leader is a person of influence, you must find ways to channel
your influence capabilities to build up others and cause positive change in whatever situation comes your way.

■ *Whatever your role of leadership, God is entrusting you with the
care of others. Give them His care.* That's the challenge for all
men as leaders—to be like Jesus of Nazareth. If you appreciate
His heart and His passion to love and serve others, then model
His life and you will live as a man of God.

■ *Intimidation always causes resentment.* Always. Bullying may
cause fear, but it yields a loss of relationship. Examine your life
for both the overt and the subtle ways that you seek to intimidate others. Ask God to give you a heart that respects and values others and watch the change in relationships.

■ *Spiritual power is given to men by God for the advancement of
the kingdom.* Incredible things can happen with men when
their lives are empowered with the Spirit of God. Ordinary
men are transformed into heroes. Such spiritual power is never
for our fame and glory, however. It is to advance the important
works God has in mind. Pray that God would give you the
spiritual power He wants to manifest in you.

■ *Words and deeds can make you a man of great influence regardless
of your position.* This is perhaps the most profound aspect of
power you can learn. Using such ordinary tools as the tele-
phone, the computer, and the spoken word, you can be a man
of incredible influence. Your words might well change your
child's life. You could tell your child, "You are a loser. You have
no potential. I wish you'd never been born." Or you can say,
"You are the most precious child I could have ever asked for. I

know God is going to do something special with you." Words of affirmation have tremendous power. Of course, affirming words should extend far beyond children. Your spouse, your coworkers—actually anyone you meet on any given day—can have a piece of their lives transformed by your influence of creating in them a sense of worth, purpose, and appreciation. Try it. You can be a man of great power—the power of influence —even this day.

Principles ... of Power

Men of passion need principles to apply when it comes to power. Here are several:

1. *A man of power is most loved and appreciated when his authority is used for the most good.* Power is misused most when we think it is about us. Our thinking must be transformed to see that power is placed in our hands for the well-being of others. As this happens, others develop a greater sense of trust and appreciation for your leadership.

2. *A man of power is most respected when he acts with wisdom, justice, and mercy.* Reckless use of power is easy to spot. It is offensive, hurtful, and prideful. But a man of wisdom who acts with justice and mercy will be revered.

3. *A man of power is most effective when he influences positive change in those he leads.* Learn to measure a healthy use of power by what happens for the good as a result. But tandem to that thinking is what happens to the people involved along the way.

4. *A man who reveres God knows that all power and might, all glory, belong to Him and to Him alone.* Regardless of what earthly power or control we may have on this earth, it pales in

comparison to the almighty God. The Bible describes it this way: "For in Christ all the fullness of the Deity lives in bodily form, and you have been given fullness in Christ, who is the head over every power and authority" (Colossians 2:9–10). Our power is finite. His is infinite.

Notes

1. Dave Barry, "Muscle-Mass Hysteria," *The Washington Post*, 3 October 2004, W32.

2. *Merriam-Webster's Collegiate Dictionary*, 10th ed., s.v. "Power"; www.merriam-webster. com/dictionary/power.

Insights on Power
. . . with Joe Stowell

Strength is all about inner stuff. You are not strong until you are strong on the inside. True power, true strength is defined in the *inner man*, not in all these kinds of macho things that our society forces on us in terms of what true strength looks like.

Jesus had that inner strength. A lot of guys look at drawings or supposed pictures of Jesus and see Him as meek and soft. You're glad He's your Savior, but you don't want to play golf with Him. But Jesus was compelling to very real men. As soon as they saw Christ, those tough, rugged fishermen—Peter, James, John, and Andrew—dropped their nets and followed Him. Then there's this shark in the marketplace—Matthew the tax collector—who could care less what people thought about him. All he wanted was to make more money on the back of somebody else. Yet Matthew followed Jesus. Simon the Zealot, a tough member of the resistance force, followed Him too.

So Christ was a genuine man. He was a man's man. And one of the things that Christ has taught us about is the legitimate use of *power*.

He also taught us about meekness. Many of us think of meekness as this doormat thing: "Oh, I've got to lie down and let my wife and my kids and people at the office—including my boss—walk all over me." Nothing could be further from the truth. Biblical meekness is the ability to give an offense to God, so that God will deal with your enemy or the person hurting you, and then loving this person in return. Meekness is one of the most powerful commodities that any man can ever possess.

Real power comes by surrendering to the Holy Spirit. Suppose I walk into a situation where I need to be courageous enough to stand up for Christ. I ask the Holy Spirit, not out of my own power but of His, "Would You now give me the courage to speak for Christ in this situation? Would You give me the words to say?" It's a matter of surrendering to the Spirit, who then directs our power in ways that bring glory to God and gain to the people around us.

Our power should be used as an *investment* in other people's lives—not to control our environment for ourselves. If you do, you will feel broken and ultimately, totally lonely. Nobody wants to be around somebody who uses power for gain against you.

To learn if your power is in balance, look at your personal encounters. How do you treat everyone you meet? How do you treat the guy who cuts you off on the freeway? How do you treat your children? Is your life geared to being a blessing . . . or to having everybody be a blessing to you? A healthy man uses his power to make good things happen.

Remember, there is power in humility. Jesus was the most humble man on this earth. He humbled Himself under God's hand and obeyed His father. He humbled Himself to serve others. The Bible says, "God resists the proud but gives grace to the humble." Grace is a *power* thing.

You ought to mess something up today just to be able to say to your wife, "You know, I was wrong. Will you please forgive me?" It's a wonderful moment. It is a power moment in a man's life.

> *Joe Stowell is author of the Gold Medallion winning book* The Trouble with Jesus, *as well as* Perilous Pursuits *and several other books. He is the past president of the Moody Bible Institute of Chicago and currently serves as Teaching Pastor of Harvest Bible Chapel in suburban Chicago.*

I count him braver who overcomes his desires than him who conquers his enemies; for the hardest victory is over self.

—Aristotle

Everyone born of God overcomes the world. This is the victory that has overcome the world, even our faith.

—1 John 5:4

4 The Passion for Winning

In 2005 I was in Chicago for a very important piece of history. The Chicago White Sox won the World Series! It was their first world championship in eighty-eight years! Meanwhile their crosstown rivals, the Cubs, still wait. Loyal Cubs fans have endured their share of pain; their last championship was in 1908.

Everyone loves a winner—and everyone loves to win. In my limited experience of coaching Little League baseball, I discovered there are not only competitive men (fathers) but also many competitive women (mothers). And since more and more women are getting into sports, we're seeing that competitive edge emerge. However, when it comes to being competitive, all genders are not equal. It is men who seem driven to compete.

Years ago as a Little League coach, I was a driven man. I wanted our teams to win! And usually, they did. But there were dads out there who wanted to win more than I did. And it showed. Sometimes in very unpleasant ways.

I quit coaching Little League because the parents got to me! Whether it was believing their kid should start over another boy or disagreement over my lineup or some game strategy, there was always a parent ready to tell me how to be a better coach. Sometimes moms, but more often dads.

I didn't have the patience to continue. But honestly, I also found that my own emotions got out of balance.

Collecting Trophies

In high school, I won a speech competition at state level and went on to the national event where I placed fifth. It bugged me. My plan was to be first! Yes, competitive drive with the passion to win is very, very strong.

Later in life, this drive to win for men will manifest itself in a lot of ways. For example, in the woman that you can show off. Some men marry very attractive women and are happy with the stares their wives receive. What do they call these beautiful women? "Trophy wives." Men also buy expensive cars to show off and convey they are successful. They try to get employed by the right company. And get the best title on the business card. Each one of these becomes a "trophy" for our manhood.

How well we do in life is often used as compelling evidence that defines who we are. And when we meet some guy who doesn't seem to have it all together, what's the general term used for a person like that? A *loser*. We may not even recognize how much identity we have at stake acting and looking like a winner.

In this chapter we're going to look at a passion that stirs deep within a man's soul: the passion for winning. By now our two objectives for studying our passions should be clear. First, if you feel these passions, you are a man! But to live life as God intended for you to live, you need to be a man in balance. And that's our second objective.

<u>Components of Winning</u>

To find the balance point, let's look at some components of this God-given passion—the passion for winning. I've chosen five word associations for this passion: *an opponent, a game plan, the engagement, crisis points,* and *a reward.* We will look at each.

An Opponent

Basic to any form of competition is the need to have *an opponent.* The opponent is the obstacle to your cause. The opponent is your adversary and is often a person. But the actual opponent might also be a significant event that has stood between you and a successful life. The opponent could be a memory. It is anything that steps between you and your success objective.

As a man, you *will* face opponents in life. Realizing this helps you overcome the idea that you can please everyone. You can't. Some opponents will never like you or approve of you. There will always be those who see the world differently than you do.

When it comes to opponents or adversaries, remember that life is a series of overcoming obstacles. And in that way, life is like running the high hurdles at a track meet. You must meet and leap the hurdles that confront you and could block your path. Being a man requires that you not attempt to avoid the obstacles, but that you handle them well.

A Game Plan

The second component in winning is to have *a game plan*—a calculated understanding of the contest and a strategy to win. In wartime generals develop battle plans. In business, founders and owners develop the business plans detailing the competition and identifying the competitive advantages. In sports, coaches use offensive and defensive schemes. In finances, it's wise to have adults develop solid financial plans. In the "game of life" there is great wisdom in having a plan.

In an outstanding video resource for men entitled, "The Quest for

Authentic Manhood," Robert Lewis challenges men to create a "manhood plan." His follow-up materials are also geared to helping men establish some clear guidelines and direction for their lives. As the saying goes, "If you don't know where you're going, any road will get you there." So life requires a game plan if you want to come out a winner.

The Engagement

A third component of winning is *the engagement*. An engagement is a deliberate attempt to remove the obstacles to defeat. Many men have a weak stomach when it comes to conflict. There are other men who absolutely love it. Trial lawyers seem to thrive on conflict. So do those collection agency phone people.

If engagement lies ahead, it's essential to weigh the strengths and weaknesses of your opponent. Confidence comes when you know you are prepared. Regardless of the kind of battle, be it physical, emotional, or spiritual, knowing the enemy's strengths and weaknesses will help you to victory.

The challenge in entering conflict is that the engagement often requires much of us emotionally. Unless you are cold-blooded, that is usually the reason people avoid conflict. It wears you out. And a man fears losing control.

During the seven years I hosted a radio talk show in Pittsburgh, almost every day included conflict or engagement on some level. It was surprising how some very articulate and under-control type people could lose it when you hit the right button.

Men face engagements on many fronts. It may be with your wife or kids. On the job. Doing battle over some community issue. Life is a series of engagements. Conflict is unavoidable.

With that in mind, it doesn't make sense for men to engage, unless it is over something worth defending and where they know being right matters. Entering into foolish controversies or engaging in conflict for "fun" is fruitless and damaging. A prudent man will avoid these things.

The Crisis Points

Winning also involves *crisis points*. A crisis point can be defined as *a zenith of energy at the height of battle upon which the outcome turns*. In the Civil War, for example, many people would say it was the battle of Gettysburg in central Pennsylvania. In sports, reporters are always trying to identify those key plays that decide a game. In business, there are deal makers and deal breakers. Your life is the same way. It will have crisis points on which things turn.

These crisis points are the foundation for building a man's character. In that sense, crisis points are good. Knowing full well that you will face these significant challenges, a man must draw from strength he has groomed in his life.

This is especially true in the area of the thought life. Many years ago I heard a pastor preaching about sexual entanglements. He pointed out that most adultery doesn't "just happen." It might begin with an innocent conversation at the water cooler or the copy machine, perhaps by just offering to help. A little casual conversation follows. And a friendly smile.

Over time, these little nuances of playfulness turn into more serious attention. Then comes the crisis point. Perhaps it's a time of life when a man is not getting the attention he feels he deserves. Or he is just vulnerable to temptation because his heart is not prepared to resist such a challenge. But the crisis point is at hand.

How will the battle turn? It depends on how well he is prepared. The reason men are encouraged to memorize Scripture as followers of Jesus is to have adequate resources to face these battles common to all men.

Seeking the Right Reward

Finally, winning involves a *reward*. After all, that's why we go into battle. Winning brings with it the spoils. It's the payoff, the trophy, the prize, the cause worth defending. It is important to examine whether the battles we are fighting in life are worth fighting.

Are you feeling defeated? Perhaps you need a new life strategy. You may need to reassign resources to a new direction or approach. Most of all, you may need a strategy to win that will leave you fulfilled. Winning builds confidence. And if you have been on a losing track, it is time to turn things around. Sometimes, men have to learn to win!

In the men's ministry in which I served, we encouraged men to celebrate often. Celebration marks important achievements and the cause of winning. Maybe you haven't had a good celebration recently. This helps keep you motivated and pressing on for the cause.

It must be said that losing is not all bad. It also shapes our character as men. And if we learn from our mistakes and losses, we can actually gain. Thirdly, we develop a sense of humility. And we can develop our resourcefulness. Losses also give us a good glimpse of who we really are. Losing . . . is a reality check.

Why God Gives a Passion to Win

These components of winning apply to all men. A man's passion for winning is among the most personal of his passions. His self-esteem rises and falls with the outcomes of his battles. Just as we talk about momentum shifting in a football game, the very same thing happens to us in life. If we get a series of defeats, we're bound to look at life more negatively. Without depth of character, a few losses could turn a man into a "loser."

That raises the question, Why did God design man with this desire for winning? Because He knew that life on this earth would be a battlefield on many levels. Our God is a God of passion and purpose and adventure. He is a God who understands victory—it is benchmarked in the resurrection of Jesus, the victor over the ultimate defeat for humans, our death. Yet in Jesus' resurrection, we have the evidence that God rules supremely over death! This is the final victory for any man whose hope is placed in the Son of God.

One of the books on the recommended reading list for this chapter is *Victory Secrets of Attila the Hun* by Wess Roberts. I found several valuable principles in this. For example, a Hun should learn early in life that not every Hun will be his or her friend. Nevertheless, a Hun who is not a friend need not be an enemy. Here's another. A Hun who doesn't confront his fears, challengers, and foes never wins. Winning past battles doesn't entitle Huns to future battle wins.

> *I would rather lose in a cause that will some day win, than win in a cause that will some day lose.*
> ■ Woodrow Wilson
>
> *"Where, O death, is your victory? Where, O death, is your sting?" . . . But thanks be to God! He gives us the victory through our Lord Jesus Christ.*
> ■ 1 Corinthians 15:55–57

Finally, chieftains whose main desire is to be liked and accepted will surely fail to achieve this goal when they must make unpopular decisions. I've had to work on that last one because of my concern over having a "nice guy" image. You know, wanting to be liked by all. In one of my early radio talk-show jobs, I allowed callers to go on and on without ending the call in a timely fashion. I was afraid to interrupt.

One day the station manager challenged me on this. He asked if I was aware that a particular call went excessively long. I admitted I did, and he asked why I let it happen. "It's hard to kind of squeeze in a word, and besides, I didn't want to offend her," I explained.

"Well, Mark, you didn't. Unfortunately, you offended everyone else who was listening and a good portion of them probably turned off their radios."

Ouch! There is always a price to be paid when we fail to engage in a matter when we know something has to be done.

The Winning Continuum

As with all of our passions, the winning continuum gives us a challenge to live a balanced life.

On this continuum, on the far left side is *the loser*—one who is either incompetent or unable to succeed. This is the man who appears doomed to fail or disappoint. Some other words that might amplify this personality are *flop*, *underdog*, *dud*, and *washout*. Ever feel like one of those? Sometimes we even hear of "the perennial loser."

The Winning Continuum

The Loser   **The Brutal Conqueror**

In Balance

On the other end of our continuum is *the brutal conqueror*. Not just your ordinary conqueror . . . this is the *brutal* conqueror. To him winning is everything! Dominating and destroying is even better. (We saw some of this in the "Passion of Power" chapter as well.) Winning in arguments, winning in relationships, sports, on the road driving . . . you name it. He *has* to win.

This man can't afford to lose. If he does, he becomes an angry man. If there is a credo for this man, it's "I'm always right, and I have to win." He is an easy spiritual target for his spiritual enemy who goads him with this simple message: You are your own God. No one should win or rule over you.

Team building is secondary. Coaching this person is nearly impossible. His emotions are out of control.

The winning basketball program at Duke University has a superb coach, Mike Krzyzewski. His attitude toward his players and the game is impressive. I'm told that "Coach K" recruits a player with this in mind: How does the player handle authority? Young men who handle authority are obviously coachable. That's a winner's attitude: wanting to win but disciplined to prepare and learn from others in order to win.

Stay on the left side of the continuum and you're in danger of missing your assignment in life to be a champion. The mind-set of a champion wants a winning environment at home and at work and wherever he serves. This man wants to make a difference. Men who lean towards a "loser" attitude can find themselves becoming lazy and uncommitted to try. This man can be unreliable. You need a "winner's adjustment."

If you lean to the other side of that spectrum, your pride may be your enemy. Coaching Little League or Pop Warner football isn't about the kids; it's about you. Anytime and anywhere you see challenge, you're compelled to win. You've come to attach winning with your self-worth. This compelling urge to win creates resentment in others because they don't always want to lose to you. Eventually, this drive to win—and not accomplishing it every time—will even cause you to resent *yourself*.

For a clear picture of this, simply look at the life of King Saul. This king seemingly had it all; he was a winning candidate no matter how you looked at him. But when young David became a greater conqueror and increasingly popular, Saul became a madman. Saul's drive for winning would cost him everything, including his kingdom.

You want to be a man in balance. This man maintains his passion for winning and accepts defeat when it occurs but not with resignation. He accepts the truth of the loss and learns from these experiences. He celebrates his victories but encourages his teammates at a time of loss. People view him as a "champion's champion." His character remains intact, win or lose.

Manhood Models

Many men have modeled this manly passion for winning. Two near the top of the list are England's great prime minister *Winston Churchill* and Moses' faithful successor, *Joshua*.

Churchill was a politician, soldier, and artist . . . and the twentieth century's most famous British leader. Although he was instinctively independent, Churchill was willing to work with any side agreeing with his goals. Why? Because he believed his goals were right. And he wanted to win.

As prime minister, Churchill presided over England during the very trying times of World War II. His words inspired his troops and the nation's citizens. "Never give in, never, never, never, never; in nothing great or small, large or petty, never give in, except to convictions of honor and good sense," he told the nation. His commitment was unwavering: "You ask what is our aim. I can answer in one word. It is victory. Victory at all costs. Victory in spite of all terrors. Victory however long and hard the road may be, for without victory, there is no survival."

The man who can drive himself further once the effort gets painful is the man who will win.
■ Roger Bannister

What good is it for a man to gain the whole world, and yet lose or forfeit his very self?
■ Luke 9:25

His words in later years revealed both his confidence and a recognition of his own brashness: "I am prepared to meet my maker. Whether my maker is prepared for the great ordeal of meeting me is another matter."

One of the greatest Israelite military leaders in all of Bible history was *Joshua*. He was Moses' military commander during the Exodus and journey to the Promised Land. He also served as one of the twelve spies sent by Moses to evaluate the land that would become the future home of his people. Only Joshua and Caleb returned from their spy journey with a very positive report. The other men saw only fortified cities and strong warriors. Their fears overpowered them (see Numbers 13:25–33). But not Joshua. He saw victory because he understood who his God was.

Winners are confident of their greatest strengths. For Joshua, that strength was God!

Facing the Enemy

Almost everything in life will have some confrontation, some crises point to it. A passion for winning gives men the opportunity to be victors. This passion is also important as men encounter the Enemy in spiritual warfare. Remember, someone is after your soul. Satan is relentless as an opponent for you. That is why as believers the greatest single asset we bring to the table is the absolute conviction that our God is going to lead us to victory. As the apostle John wrote, "Everyone born of God overcomes the world. This is the victory that has overcome the world, even our faith" (1 John 5:4).

> *Be self-controlled and alert. Your enemy the devil prowls around like a roaring lion looking for someone to devour.*
> ■ 1 Peter 5:8

Two final thoughts: First, remember that all men are fueled by the energy that is derived by winning. Be sure to find ways to celebrate victories. They spur us on to other things, great things. Second, recognize that all around you are men who may have experienced loss and defeat. They may still be hurting. Help them. Both inside and outside the church are men who have experienced a great deal of loss, whether it's through job, rejection, divorce, or some other loss. We're called to be ministers of the gospel to people during such losses.

Takeaways

The man on the right kind of quest for winning wants to have the heart and mind-set of a champion. These concepts can assist you in developing that:

- *Competition is healthy.* It breeds a challenge to steadily improve ourselves and the situations that we face. Regardless of our winning percentage, the effort alone to compete will almost always contribute to some improvement. It also acts as a quality filter that can be of great value.

- *Whatever battle you face, play hard, play fair, play to win.* We live in an age where some would say that winning is not a vital part of competition. But it is! Seeking to achieve your goal is a worthy cause. To excel in competition and face the risk of winning or losing is a noble quest.

- *Champions use one win to build to another. Use your small victories to advance into bigger challenges.* Regardless of the type of competition, it is true that success breeds success. When you have experienced some defeat in life, look to develop a change in the direction toward winning. Start small and work up.

- *Remember, life is a team sport. Be sure you are coaching others to greatness.* Become a master encourager to those around you and you will find your success is enhanced. The principle of giving others due credit will show that you are confident of your own abilities.

■ *Losing is temporary.* William Macy failed at his first seven attempts to establish his department store. It took his eighth before he could make it work. Zig Ziglar offers up this unusual advice: "Anything worth doing, is worth doing . . . poorly. Until you learn to do it well." Now that is a creative and powerful reminder!

Principles . . . of Winning

As you develop your thinking toward this passion for winning, consider these principles:

1. *A man passionate about winning develops his skills and his gifts with an eye on personal excellence.* The man who really wants to win knows he must pursue excellence. That's not just doing his best; it's also being deeply committed to the best.

2. *A man passionate about winning keeps his character intact, whether celebrating victory or enduring defeat.* Character is as important to a coach as the outcome, and a good player knows that character counts.

3. *A man passionate about winning will use sacrifice and discipline as measuring devices of this pursuit.* Ask yourself, "Am I willing to pay the price?" Discipline means waking up when you don't want to wake up; to continue to practice and improve.

4. *A man in pursuit of great victory, especially your eternal one, does not underestimate the Enemy, who is relentless.* The soul is his battleground, and his approach often is aggressive. As long as you live, Satan will be there. Learn to respect him as an enemy, but know that you have a victory to claim (see 1 John 4:4).

Note

1. The Quest for Authentic Manhood is a video series designed for a twenty-four-session study on issues of manhood, including a man's core identity.

Insights on Winning
. . . with Bill McCartney

Green Bay Packers Coach Vince Lombardi once said, "Winning isn't everything, it is the only thing." In a sense, yes, he was right, because Scripture tells us that we are to run to win. We're not to be shadow boxing.

The verse in Scripture that captures this for me is Colossians 3:23 when Paul writes, "Whatever you do, do it with all your heart." But, and this is the key, "Do it for the Lord, rather than for man" (author paraphrase). In other words, what is your motive? Paul tells the people of Corinth that our motive is to receive "an imperishable crown." Motives define why we do what we do.

In the Christian faith, we've got a picture in our hearts of what God has promised us. That becomes our motivation. So winning is very important, but in the context the sports legend used, no, he was not right.

Most men have a strong competitive nature. That's a healthy part of our God-given design. Iron sharpens iron. We need each other. My spiritual gift is found in Romans 12:8 (NASB). It is exhortation. That is one kind of spiritual gift. And this gift works inside or outside the kingdom. When I coached, it was my strongest asset. And it's also a blessing to me as a brother in Christ with other brothers. Yeah, you need competitive people. *The most competitive people play the most competitive games.*

A weak man makes others around him weak. A weak father in the home makes everybody in the home weaker. A strong, faithful father makes everyone in the home stronger. It is true that many men lack discipline. They lack commitment. They lack resolve. In Deuteronomy 20:8 (NASB) we discover, "Who is the man that is afraid and fainthearted? Let him depart and return to his house, so that he might not make his brothers' hearts melt like his heart."

Jesus said that whoever would come after Him must do two things: He must deny himself and take up his cross. Basically, he's got to have the fire. He's got to have resolve. If a man is just a humble guy, you'll be attracted to him but you won't follow him. On the other hand, if a guy has great resolve, you'd be attracted to him, but he'll wear you out. It's that balance that Christ wants.

Men are out of balance if winning is an obsession. Generally speaking, men who can't handle losing are control guys. Their identity is wrapped up in what they are *doing* and not who they *are*. Deep down, these men are fearful. They are driven. In fact, they are some of the most strong, driven men out there. Some are control freaks. I've walked in and out of that path of these men when I coached. You know, I have to take responsibility and say sometimes *I coached like that*. And I repent over that.

Your spiritual senses have to be matured. Do you hear the voice of God? Do you taste and discern the will of God? Do you have the sweet fragrance of those who are full of life? Your spiritual maturity is wrapped up in that. The "breastplate of righteousness" is about the heart. And there's more to the armor, as we are told in the Bible. Put those things on.

To win on the battlefield of life, men must help men. The clearest and most positive way Promise Keepers has helped has been to assist men in forming accountability groups. They bond. I heard someone say that women bond face-to-face. But men bond *shoulder to shoulder* when they take on a challenge together. Accountability groups have helped men take on challenges together.

I believe after men hear an inspiring message, they get motivated. And for two, three, or four days in a row, they get out of bed and they get on their knees. It's dark out. They go before the Lord and they cry out to Him . . . and nothing happens. And so they stop doing it. That is why they fall in an apathetic condition.

For men to be winners, they need to know He is there. When they find themselves out there in the morning all by themselves reaching out, He's there. He promises to be there. He cannot . . . *not be there*. His word is good.

So keep going after Him until you find Him. Keep reaching out to Him until He answers you. An extraordinary bond develops, and you will really get to know God. But men don't stay after Him. They don't persevere. If God doesn't show up right away or in a day or two, then they're out of Dodge. Men must be challenged to hang in there to win!

> *Bill McCartney founded Promise Keepers, an organization dedicated to encouraging and discipling godly men. A successful head football coach at the University of Colorado, he left that pinnacle to spend more time with his family and begin the PK men's movement.. Recently he founded The Road to Jerusalem, a mission for Christians to embrace the Messianic Jewish community.*

We make a living by what we get,
but we make a life by what we give.

—Winston Churchill

■

If you give, you will receive. Your
gift will return to you in full
measure, pressed down, shaken
together to make room for more,
and running over. Whatever measure
you use in giving—large or small—
it will be used to measure what
is given back to you.

—Luke 6:38 (NLT)

5 The Passion for Wealth

When I was sixteen years old, my father passed away. He was fifty-five. His death left my mother and me alone at home, as my sisters were older and had already moved out. My mother did not have a job at the time.

In his final five years, my father had suffered several business set-backs, including a donut shop he sold to his partner when the partner wanted to run the business on his own. Then my father became an insurance salesman . . . until he got a call from his former partner asking to be rescued. This young man was in over his head. My father reentered the business only to find conditions worse than he had been told. He had to close the shop a year later with heavy debts over our family.

When the donut business failed, the partner filed bankruptcy and got somewhat of a fresh start. My father chose to pay off creditors any way he could, even by borrowing money wherever he could to make this happen. So the remainder of his life was dedicated to getting our family out of debt. It may well have cost my father more than he bargained for . . . his life. It was a stressful period of time.

Unfortunately for our family, my father died without a life

insurance policy. We rented a home. We had no savings. There were no rich relatives on which to fall back. We were, essentially, penniless. Social Security provided a meager income for my mother. I worked part-time while going to school. Yet God, as He often does, provided in ways we never fully understand. His heart for the widow is strong.

Although I have managed money slightly better than my father, raising three children and sending them off to college has been an expensive proposition. Along the way, we used credit cards to support their habits—of buying clothing, school supplies and activities they simply had to be involved in. Those kids' college loans still haunt us.

There are many poor managers of wealth. If you meet a man of means, don't assume he has his act together. A friend of mine has a business that helps the wealthy develop and implement a financial legacy. Several years ago, he created a "wealth loss scorecard" that listed the names of several prominent people who had *lots* of money. On the scorecard were multiple choice answers listing the percentage of their wealth that remained in their estate after their passing. It was *shockingly low* in several cases. These were people like Elvis Presley, J. P. Morgan, Henry Kaiser, and the Rockefellers.

Most men have a passion for wealth. I've never met a man who wouldn't appreciate having more. I've met many a man for whom this passion defines their lives—and not enough men who see wealth for its greatest intended purpose.

If you are a man who is driven to build and grow and earn, you are living out the assignment God gave you on this earth. He put us in charge of affairs on this planet, and God wants to see things grow. It is a manly passion.

But men of passion also need to be men of balance. A man whose drive for wealth is out of control can do great damage . . . and be a Scrooge as a person. A man in balance will understand both the pitfalls and the benefits to worldly wealth. We will look at that in a moment.

The Components of Wealth

There are five important components of wealth: *accumulation, your spending nature, quality preference, stewardship,* and *philanthropy.*

Accumulation

Accumulation is the act of increasing the amount or the value of something owned. Perhaps nothing reveals the challenge of accumulating "stuff" more than the booming public storage business. In the Midwest, we have basements. In many of the newer developments, we have three-car garages. Yet with a third garage and a full basement, some homeowners *still* have to rent a storage facility!

The United States is a culture of accumulation. Despite our bigger houses and significant space beyond what our grandparents or great-grandparents ever considered, we seem to need more room.

In my neighborhood, each person has a lawnmower and most have gardening equipment, such as leaf blowers and weed whackers. All of it gets used once a week, if that. And yet every guy must have his own! What does that tell you? It tells me that we want our own stuff.

> *The world offers only the lust for physical pleasure, the lust for everything we see, and pride in our possessions. These are not from the Father. They are from this evil world.*
> ■ 1 John 2:16 (NLT)

The Spending Nature

The second component of wealth is our *spending nature* or *habits.* Each of us has certain approaches toward making a purchase. There is the comparison shopper versus the impulse buyer. Most of us fall into the second category. In fact, impulse buying drives a lot of the American economy. Sam Walton, founder of Wal-Mart, knew it. That's why when you go into Wal-Mart you see center aisles stacked up with stuff. That's why when you go to a grocery checkout, they have all those little overpriced items, snacks, and gum staring at you. It's all impulse stuff.

Even a comparison shopper might not buy out of need. If it is on sale or seems like a convenient item, he may buy even if he doesn't need it. Often we buy because of convenience or sale prices.

Men tend not to have this disease in the same way women do. By that I mean most men do not enjoy spending hours shopping at malls or stores. Of course, Home Depot or Lowe's may be a different story. Men may not be into clothing or decorating, but they often want the latest and the best, especially when it comes to technology and tools.

The real issue here is to recognize that we do have certain spending styles that impact our lives in ways we may not seriously consider. For families heavily in debt and unable to save any money, these tendencies are worth looking at. Controls need to be in place.

Quality Preference

Quality preference is another component of wealth. When someone purchases something of lasting value, she demonstrates a quality preference. Most really wealthy people share something in common: the lack of junk. Many upscale homes are very simply decorated, and what is used to decorate is chosen by its quality.

You say you aren't wealthy? Well, keep in mind that you demonstrate quality preference when you look to purchase an item of exceptional value. Garage sales and clearance sales are two famous examples. Some look for great values through Internet sales and auctions. My sister makes a living on eBay. She knows the kind of quality items or collectibles that people want most. She bought and then sold an ugly green monkey for a remarkable profit. I would have burned it.

So value shopping is when quality and bargain buying go hand in hand. A good money manager understands value.

Stewardship

Stewardship is the fourth component of wealth. A steward manages the resources owned by someone else. If you are a follower of Jesus, it is this core belief that you are a steward of God's resources that should cause you to live differently in attitude and action when it comes to wealth. Said another way, *God owns it all.* Regrettably, far too many people who claim the cause of Christ maintain a personal ownership mind-set that treats possessions and wealth as if they were their own. They spend vast sums on themselves and miss the opportunities God has for them to live generously.

If we truly embraced the belief that God owns it all and that we are the stewards of His resources, the world would change, for true stewards look at the big picture; and there are enough resources on this planet to manage the needs of all the inhabitants. God has entrusted His resources into your care, for your needs and the needs of others.

However, it is common to think that our skill and prowess makes the difference instead of God's blessing. We must not take credit for outcomes and attribute brilliance to ourselves, thus saying, "I am entitled to my success!" That is a heart attitude that requires a humbling before God and a decision to honor Him with what He has given us. Remember, God entrusts more to people who are good stewards. God wants you to see Him—not yourself—as the provider.

Philanthropy

The final component under wealth is *philanthropy.* When at Christmas we echo the angels and say, "Peace on earth and good will toward men" (see Luke 2:14), we are challenging each other to be philanthropic in our hearts. Americans have good reasons to be generous. Our government gives us tax breaks!

However, studies I have seen of church giving indicate that we are running very low percentage-wise on "good will toward men." Thinking that the government has the responsibility to care for the needs of the poor is *not* charitable giving. Our country thrives on the opportunity for individuals to succeed. Our faith is likewise an individual matter. We must not think that being part of a church gets us to heaven. We must connect to God personally. Charity must be a personal choice as well.

Being a good steward means making your contribution; it's *your* sacrifice that makes the difference. Men, don't consider yourself a generous person if you simply want to give somebody else's money away. Think first of being a good steward of your resources. Determine what sacrifices you are willing to make.

A Passion That Men Protect

A man's passion for wealth is among his most personally protected of passions. Pastors are often afraid to preach on this subject. It's one sermon that makes people very uncomfortable—handling money!

The great risk of having much is feeling secure without regard for God. Jesus addressed that in a statement about it being "easier for a camel to go through the eye of a needle than for a rich man to enter the kingdom of God" (Mark 10:25). Wealth can allow us to think we do not need our Creator.

So why did God design man with a desire to accumulate? Because He is the giver of all good things and His character is to give generously. And He created you in His image. He wants you to reflect Godlike character. For more on this topic, consider the recommended reading materials at the end of this book.

The Wealth Continuum

We can check our balance on this subject on the continuum of wealth. At the far left of the continuum is *the big spender*. This is the man who spends imprudently or wastefully, someone who is not to be trusted with large sums of money. When out of balance, this person by "excessive drinking, gaming, idleness, or debauchery . . . shall spend, waste, or lessen his estate as to expose himself or his family to want or to suffering."[1] This man cannot hold on to a dollar. It's gone before he knows it.

Most family trusts try to protect against the excesses of the big spender. The inheritance typically includes a clause that prevents beneficiaries from assigning their trust interest or creditors from seizing the funds from that trust for the big spender's foolish debts. Good financial managers don't want to hand over their assets to reckless people.

At the other end of that continuum is *the miser:* the greedy person, the covetous, grasping person—one who lives meagerly and miserably for the sake of saving and increasing his hoarded money and possessions. Other terms we use include *hoarder, cheapskate, glutton,* and *money-grubber.*

To be a godly man, you want to be in balance as a good steward. If you're on the left side as a big spender, even if you won the lottery, that money would soon dwindle and be eaten away by your foolish spending. A big spender should not expect God to entrust him with much. If you lean that direction, you need a course in how to manage your money and a mentor to teach you about spending.

If you recognize yourself as being closer to the miser, you are withholding good things from others. It's very possible that you're vastly under-giving for kingdom purposes. If that is the case, you also cannot expect God's reward in this life, certainly not crowns in the life to come. You need a heart change, to ask God to give you *His* heart toward wealth and resources.

Manhood Models

These short glimpses of good stewardship teach us much about what can be done with the right heart or attitude.

John Wesley, an itinerant preacher in England, rode two hundred and fifty thousand miles on horseback, preached forty thousand sermons, and gave thirty thousand pounds away. That's a lot of money —a prosperous farmer of his day could expect to earn no more than one hundred and fifty pounds a year. Some say Wesley gave away about 80 percent of the money that he earned.

Throughout his life, he identified himself and his movement with outcasts of society. He told one correspondent in 1757, "I love the poor. In many of them I find pure, genuine grace unmixed with paint [make-up], folly and affectation."[2] John Wesley was committed to the cause of realizing that God blessed him with finances and with wealth and accumulation in order that he might be a world-changer.

Money is like manure; it's not worth a thing unless it's spread around, encouraging young things to grow.
■ Thornton Wilder

The blessing of the LORD makes a person rich, and he adds no sorrow with it.
■ Proverbs 10:22 (NLT)

Sam Walton is another worthy model. The founder of Wal-Mart started in retailing with the JC Penney Company as an eighty-five-dollar-a-month trainee. He spent a few years working for Penney's and soon observed an opportunity to help consumers through what later became known as "five-and-dime" stores. He bought a Ben Franklin discount store, and eventually Sam and other family members owned sixteen variety stores, including fifteen Ben Franklins.

He pioneered several innovations, including moving checkout registers to the front of the stores (instead of scattering them in various departments) and negotiating volume discounts with suppliers. Eventually Walton decided to build large discount supercenters.[3] And the rest, as they say, is history.

In 1990, they had more than a thousand stores and one hundred and fifty thousand employees. Wal-Mart has tripled since that time and has ten times the employees![4] Its charitable arm, the Walton Foundation, has given over $300 million alone to the University of Arkansas. I don't know about Sam's personal heart toward philanthropy, but he was a man who understood sacrifice and the opportunities created by accumulation. Though wealthy, Sam Walton drove an old car instead of a Mercedes. He didn't have to have a ten-car garage or an enormous estate. He lived pretty frugally. While some might assume he was all about money, Walton showed a different side.

Acting on a God-Given Assignment

A man who is passionate about multiplying his efforts and investments has acted on a God-given assignment for a man. That's what men are supposed to do. Go out and build, develop, and grow. When you have this kind of passion, you are living a manly vision.

Followers of Christ need to be role models in the world of wealth. You can be a world-changer for one person, a family, a ministry, a cause. One person can make an enormous difference because of finances. A man who commits to using his wealth to improve the world for others has a godly passion.

In reading this chapter, you have made an investment yourself.

An investment of time. Perhaps this chapter will change your outlook on wealth. And in the process, it may change the world a bit. Begin with your son; be sure to inform him, and then pass it on to others. That would be my prayer.

Takeaways

Men who wonder about wealth should take to heart these truths:

- *God blesses His creation by enabling men and women to have and accumulate. He meets our needs in order that we might help meet the needs of others.* Have you considered and truly thanked God for your blessings? Thank Him not only with your words but by your actions. Prove your beliefs by your deeds.

- *American leaders do not encourage enough sacrifice, control of debt, or building of reserves. You must learn these financial disciplines on your own.* Perhaps it was done decades ago, but you just don't hear politicians with passion telling Americans to save more, budget carefully, and build a future for themselves and others. We may hear a platitude about America being a generous land. But you don't hear a speech challenging Americans to control debt and spending and to invest. Practice financial discipline by avoiding large debt and saving for the future.

- *A heart of compassionate giving is a proactive decision.* Don't expect to wake up one morning and find that you are more generous. Instead, you must decide and plan to be that kind of person. When you hear of personal needs of friends or relatives and when you receive those requests from ministries and charitable organizations, it is decision time. Be proactive with your decisions, and such giving will become habit.

- *A prudent financial manager with a heart for God lends liberally and avoids overindulgence in keeping up with the Joneses.* A man who has made wise financial choices, such as avoiding significant debt to indulge himself, can use his resources to assist many others in getting on a solid financial footing. Trying to keep up with the Joneses is an impossible goal. Somewhere there is a Jones family that can always outspend you.

■ *A secret to being rich: If rich means having everything you could want, reduce your wants.* That statement almost sounds like someone is playing with our minds. But my longtime friend Al Bass shared it with me years ago. Al spends time with kids at a camp every summer. Apparently, he noticed his campers were excessively interested in the material things of life. And so he offered some kind of reward if they would answer the question, "How would you define being rich?" The kids had many answers, of course, but Al got them to agree that being rich meant being able to have everything you want. And he said, "Here's the secret to being rich: Reduce your wants."

■ *The prosperity gospel is a false gospel.* We don't give to get. We give expecting nothing in return. The church—those who embrace the heart and teachings of Jesus—is embarrassed by preachers of this false gospel. This "gospel" is not about giving and sacrifice in order to honor God, it's about giving . . . to get! That is not the gospel of Jesus. His followers need to learn to give, expecting nothing in return.

Principles . . . of Wealth

For a man to live as a good steward of wealth, he must develop his own set of guiding principles. Here are a few to think about:

1. *A man passionate about providing for his family and the well-being of others—the lives he touches most—is pursuing noble ends.* A man should care deeply about providing for his family as

well as for others. This is a worthwhile ambition and is basic to manly living.

2. *A man who is generous with his wealth for others to see but who has no heart for true giving and does it only for show, fails to impress God.* The Bible makes clear reference to this. Jesus once observed the giving that took place outside of the temple. At that time, coins were the means of exchange, and when those coins were dropped into the collection buckets, they made noise! Small coins had their own sounds to them. One poor widow gave all she had. It wasn't much. But Jesus praised her for her devotion while others gave only out of their abundance (see Luke 21:1–4). If you give only out of your abundance—or simply to avoid taxes—you may not truly be a generous person.

3. *A man whose lifestyle is held in check so that he may honor God with his giving is a man wise in stewardship.* This is a key reason for having limits on our desires. How much is enough? A wise steward readily recognizes that wealth can consume him and that a man's desires are unquenchable. With that in mind, he keeps himself from peril by being purposeful in establishing controls.

4. *A wise man realizes that winning the lottery is not a financial plan.* It might take a "minimum investment" but it has incredibly low returns. A good steward finds betters ways to generate a return on the dollar than gambling.

Notes

1. *Law Dictionary,* s.v. "Spendthrift," based on the revised statute of Vermont, tit. 16, c. 65, s. 9; http://www.law-dictionary.org/?q=spendthrift.

2. "British Methodism and the Poor, 1739–1999," http://rylibweb.man.ac.uk/data1/dg/methodist/poor/.

3. "Sam Walton," Wikipedia, http://en.wikipedia.org/wiki/Sam_Walton.

4. Wal-Mart had 34,000 stores in the United States and 1.2 million U.S. employees as of January 2004. "Is Wal-Mart Good for America?" *Frontline,* PBS-TV; www.pbs.org/wgbh/pages/frontline/shows/secrets/stats.html.

Insights on Wealth
. . . *with Dave Ramsey*

When it comes to having financial security, most American families don't bother to make it happen. That's the biggest financial problem in America. Most Americans wander through life like Gomer Pyle; you know, "Shazaam! I'm at retirement and I'm broke. Hope the government [which is well known for its ability to handle money] will take care of me." This is not a plan.

I think it is laziness. When I got into a financial problem and lost everything I owned, that was *my* problem. I wasn't bothering to be proactive in the situation, to make the money behave. Combine a little bit of short-term thinking—definition "immaturity"—with the most aggressively marketed product in our culture today, the credit card, multiplied by the number of advertising impressions that flash in front of our faces everyday. Put four or five of these little items together and you've got a financial disaster known as the average American family.

Most couples break down on the money issue because it's hard to combine two different value systems. Usually, the spender marries the saver. And two people just alike seldom get married. Larry Burkett used to say if two people just alike get married, one of them is unnecessary. And so what happens is that all these opposite things that were cute when we were dating become major issues in our relationship around the table of money.

Money fights and money problems are the number one cause of divorce in America today. That's the bad news. The good news is that we can set out to purposefully handle money together and bring our value system into oneness. You see, when we agree on spending, we agree on our dreams, on our passions, on our goals. (Jesus said your treasure is where your heart is.) And when we agree on all these things, we reach a level of unity and oneness that we get no other way. So it is a powerful issue in marriage to start handling money together.

My goal as a Christian is to try to figure out what Scripture says about all areas of my life. Now, God hasn't said anything good about debt in the Bible.

Yes, the Bible doesn't say that debt is a sin, and it doesn't say you're going to hell if you run up your credit card balances. This is not a salvation issue. But I look for guidelines on how to live particular parts of my life, like financial or health or relationships or things from Scripture, because that's my heavenly Father's love letter to me on how to live my life. And so, since I don't find anything good in there about debt, I don't do debt.

Some men think that spending a little money at the casino or playing the lottery can get you a windfall. I'm sorry; I just don't get gambling. I mean, if throwing money away is fun, why not just roll down your window as you're driving to work and throw some hundred-dollar bills out on the interstate just to cause a wreck or something? I mean, let's *really* have some fun! The idea in the lottery that *somebody's going to win* is the great lie. You know, smart people who can do math really don't play the lottery, and they don't gamble because they know that the house wins.

The key error most men make regarding the handling of their finances is indulging pleasure. We men should be delaying pleasure. We're driving along the street and all of a sudden our car just involuntarily turns into a car lot. And boom, the car fever sets in, which is when all of your brain cells don't fire against each other well and you go and buy something you totally can't afford. And so we live without a plan. We live without a direction, and we don't make our purchases as part of an overall game plan. I'm not one of these financial guys who says you can't have stuff. I'm convinced our heavenly Father wants us to enjoy money, but we are told time and time again, all through Proverbs, to have a plan. Jesus said it Himself: "Don't build a tower without first counting the cost."

Dave Ramsey made lots of money and lost it all through big debt. He got himself out of debt by establishing sound financial principles, and eventually he wrote Financial Peace. *Today, Dave's company employs about a hundred team members, and another book,* The Total Money Makeover, *remains a best seller.*

The time to take counsel of your fears is before you make an important battle decision. That's the time to listen to every fear you can imagine! When you have collected all the facts and fears and made your decision, turn off all your fears and go ahead!

—General George S. Patton Jr.

■

The thief comes only to steal and kill and destroy; I came that they may have life, and have it abundantly.

—John 10:10 (NASB)

6 The Passion for Self-Preservation

One of the most beautiful train rides in North America is the journey between Sacramento, California, and Reno, Nevada. (Railroaders tell me there is only one more spectacular ride, and it is in Canada.) As you travel on that train over the famed Donner Pass, the spectacular views almost take your breath. In winter the Amtrak train travels through the snow tunnel "sheds" with snow-covered mountains above and the deep blue Truckee Lake several hundred feet below. I've taken that trip by train several times. It has a sense of romance to it as well.

But Donner Pass is also a deadly piece of real estate. The story of the Donner Party is chronicled in a memorial near Truckee Lake. Back in November 1847, a group of migrants bound for California with wagons, horses, and families became trapped in the rugged High Sierras that straddle Nevada and California.

Here is how one newspaper reported the drama:

> *Since [the group tried] to get over the pass there in the middle of November, we have heard nothing of the company until last week when a messenger was sent down from Captain William Johnson's settlement with*

the astounding information that five women and two men had arrived at that point [almost] naked, their feet frost bitten, and then four of them with the company arrived within three miles of the small log cabin near Trucky's Lake [now called Truckee Lake] on the east side of the mountains. And they found the snow so deep that they could not travel. . . . Fearing starvation, sixteen of the strongest, eleven males and five females, agreed to start for the settlement on foot. Scantily clothed and provided with provisions, they commenced that horrid journey over the mountains that Napoleon's feat on the Alps was child's play compared with.

After wandering about a number of days, bewildered in the snow, their provisions gave out, and long hunger made it necessary to resort to that horrid recourse, casting lots to see who would give up life that their bodies might be used for food for the remainder. But at this time, the weaker began to die, which rendered it unnecessary to take life.[1]

And so, those living resorted to eating the dead in an effort to survive.

Eighty-six men, women, and children, including nine families and seventeen single men, had left Illinois for California as part of the western migration; forty-one would die. George Donner and his brother Jacob brought their families; the four parents died, as did most of the Donner children.[2]

It is difficult to imagine anything more desperate for a man's survival than to have to deal with what these people faced in trying to get over that mountain pass. And yet the reality is that when it comes to preserving life, men and women will find themselves willing to do virtually anything in order to live.

As a small boy living in Seattle, I loved to visit nearby Carkeek Park, just minutes by car from our home. Our family would enter the park by descending a winding road over a steep wooded hillside with steep ravines. The picnic and play areas were fun; so was the pedestrian bridge across railroad tracks that paralleled a sandy beach on the Puget Sound.

When I was about six years old, we joined a group from my dad's office for a picnic at Carkeek Park. Several of us kids decided to explore those wooded hillsides. After climbing a bit, I lagged behind the older kids and stopped to look down the hill to where the railroad tracks were located. It was a steep decline.

Then, in the wet soil, my feet slipped. I started to slide down that hill, grabbing at tree roots or plants or anything that might stop me. I slid only a few feet before being able to grab on to something to hold me. But I was caught—a hundred feet above the railroad tracks and no way to climb up.

Hanging On

Hanging tightly from the side of that hill, I remember looking down and thinking that this very possibly could be the end of my life— at six years old! My untrained survival skills were managed only by sheer terror.

I screamed for help, but the others seemed to have gone too far ahead to hear me. My situation was perilous, to be sure. After another minute or so of screaming for help, some people closer by heard my wailing and came to rescue me.

That was my first vivid recollection of self-preservation. Unlike Indiana Jones or super agent James Bond, most men are not in life-threatening situations each day. Instead, most men practice self-preservation of another form. We learn that we have to protect ourselves in order to function successfully in the world. We want to protect our self-image, create a perception that we are successful and capable of achievement. We are on the watch for anything that threatens our well-being in this regard. After all, "It's a jungle out there." But what kind of jungle is it? The kind where people "scratch and claw their way to the top."

There are other kinds of survival skills men must employ today. There is the challenge of understanding and completing the job. There's the challenge of women and surviving a marriage . . . and perhaps surviving the arrival of teenagers in the home. We have stress in our lives demanding more than we can give as men. Yes, we all have our personal jungles, and we're driven by self-preservation to protect our lives from the attackers of this world.

What Men . . . and Women . . . Need

Psychologist Abraham Maslow developed a theory called "The Hierarchy of Needs." Maslow wrote that human beings are motivated by unsatisfied needs and that certain lower needs must be met before higher needs can be satisfied. Maslow studied exemplary people such as Albert Einstein, Jane Addams, Eleanor Roosevelt, and Frederick Douglas rather than mentally ill or neurotic people. He concluded that there were these various "need" steps in life. The needs had to be met at the bottom first before you could move up.

Many accept this "Hierarchy of Needs" model, which begins with our physiological need to survive. Our physiological needs include air, water, food, and sleep. You know, the basics. When these needs are not met, we may feel sickness, pain, or discomfort. These were the compelling needs that members of the Donner Party faced. The need for survival drove them to do what was necessary.

The second level, which people seek only after the first level is met, is *safety* needs. Safety needs reflect our need for stability and consistency in our chaotic world. These needs are mostly psychological in nature. We need the security of a home. We need the security of family. Obviously, if there is a dysfunctional family with an abusive husband, a wife cannot move on to the next level because she doesn't have these basic safety needs met. Likewise, if you grew up with an abusive parent, it was bound to affect your sense of survival.

After these two fundamental needs, Maslow argued, each person has a need for *love and belonging*.

Next Maslow considered the need for *esteem* (both self-esteem, which results from competence, and esteem from the recognition by others), and finally the need for *self-actualization*, the desire to become more and more what one is intended to be. As he interpreted it, Maslow believed this was a point of great satisfaction for each man once he determined his purpose or role in life.

What Jesus Says about Self-Preservation

The theory of a hierarchy of needs is a very organized and interesting way to consider how we humans are wired. Maslow was a humanist. As we consider God's design for a man, I would suggest we use God's wisdom about self-preservation. So we will apply the mind of another rather famous thinker and teacher, Jesus of Nazareth.

Jesus' teachings direct us toward a different kind of priority system. His words taught that our basic needs are to be met by God. In fact, Jesus even said not to worry about what we eat or drink or wear. He explained that our heavenly Father knows what we need and is quite capable of providing it (see Matthew 6:25–33).

Jesus further taught that we cannot control the outcome of our lives. He said that "whoever wants to save his life will lose it" (Mark 8:35). Well, that is an unusual way to approach self-preservation. Even more controversial, Jesus demonstrated an *abandonment of self-preservation* in His own life, by giving up His life voluntarily and encouraging His followers to be willing to do the same.

Sometimes the messages of Jesus and Maslow's hierarchy of needs collide. Even for Christians, we find ourselves battling fear, pain, stress, anger, and pressure. We define it most often in our culture as stress. Who among us wants to live with fear, anxiety, and pain? At times, Christians find themselves doing what the world does to deal with pain, turning to alcohol or to prescription drugs. They do so to ease their pain. In the case of prescribed medications, they may do so also to prolong life (true self-preservation).

This self-preservation instinct exists, and it seems particularly strong for younger men. It can diminish as we grow older, in part because we know there is a final moment to our lives.

Let's inspect the components of this vital passion, and then evaluate ourselves for balance in the self-preservation continuum.

Components of Self-Preservation

Basic Needs

Component number one for self-preservation is *basic needs*. The Maslow hierarchy tells us what we need to know here: Food, water, shelter, and clothing are all vital. (Well, some men might make a strong case for a new Ford Mustang.) Basic needs are really survival needs.

For some men, these needs seem in jeopardy. Depending on their location and mission, our military men can be put in harm's way. During boot camp, survival training is a part of every soldier's training. Other men choose professions where survival concerns are part of the job: think firefighters and coal miners, emergency and rescue personnel.

Identity

The second component of self-preservation is *identity*, that is, establishing a healthy perspective of self and the value of being a person. Self-actualizing captures the concept well. Here's the question that men ask privately: "How do I measure up?" Put another way, "Where is my fit in the world? What value do I bring?" Every boy growing to be a man wants the answers to those questions. A man needs to know that he matters on this earth.

Emotional Survival

Component number three is *emotional survival.* As we get older, we discover the world is not a safe place. As businesses close and corporations downsize, we may lose our jobs. Health issues creep up. We can lose friends and family through estrangement or even death. Many men lose their excitement for life they had as boys; they grow up to face the real-world question: Does it matter whether I live?

A man can find himself without hope. We each have a "hope meter" within. Through various ways, that hope meter goes up and down. Long periods of frustration, stress, or seemingly impossible circumstances can bring the hope meter down to dangerous levels.

If you're a person with a faith in God, you have a reasoned hope for eternity! That should maintain a good level in our hope meters. But it doesn't always work that way for men, even men of faith. And that's why it's so important to keep a group of men around you that can help encourage you along the way with your hope meter.

> *Having chosen our course, without guile and with pure purpose, let us renew our trust in God, and go forward without fear and with manly hearts.*
> ■ Abraham Lincoln

Find a trusted friend and let him know what you are going through. Build relationships with a few men that you can count on. Listen to each other. Pray for each other. This brings balance to your circumstances and perspective as a child of God. Your hope meter for self-preservation need not run out.

Protected Care

Next in our components is *protected care.* This means putting your own self-interest aside to care for a loved one, even when serious consequences may result. You may have come along pretty far in life without any serious issues. Your basic needs have been met, and you have your identity secure, and your emotional concerns are under control. But you now have a family and what is beginning to matter most is their well-being.

In December 2005, a Southwest Airlines jet landing during a snowstorm at Chicago's Midway Airport skidded off a runway and slid through a final barrier at the end of the airfield, stopping in the middle of a city street. Remarkably, only a couple of vehicles tangled with the plane at a very busy time of the rush hour. Yet one of those two vehicles was trapped under a jet engine. The family inside survived —everyone but six-year-old Joshua Woods. The father desperately called out repeatedly to his son, but there was silence.[3]

That is protective care. A parent will do virtually anything to save a child. That same kind of attitude causes husbands to look for causes for the infamous unknown sounds in the middle of the night. Men assume this protective role.

Sacrificial Love

Our last component takes this protective care a step further. It becomes *sacrificial love.* Sometimes a man will sacrifice greatly to make the lives of others better, even when his own well-being suffers. Fully developed, this is a life abandoned to self and motivated to serve others regardless of cost. If you've reached this level of human existence, you've passed most people on the human spectrum. These are people who give their lives to make other lives matter.

Jesus of Nazareth lived this way and modeled it for us. His life was given for others. And that band of disciples of Jesus then formed a unique and elite group where they were willing to lose their lives on behalf of eternity.

Giving Our Lives for Others

Instinctively, a man has this passion to live. The passion for self-preservation is the most difficult to put aside, but that is precisely what Jesus calls us to do.

Why does God challenge men to give up their lives for others? Because life is His greatest gift to us. Eternal life is His promise for our faith. Nothing speaks louder that you believe what He said and did for you than your willingness to put your life aside.

Putting the needs of others above our own goes deep into the heart of man. It is a man putting his agenda and his priorities on the line. If you are willing to do this, then you can understand what Jesus meant by taking up your cross daily to follow Him.

The Self-Preservation Continuum

We need to find the balance point on the self-preservation continuum, the balance between *the coward* and *the daredevil.*

On the left side of the continuum is *the coward.* Like the Cowardly Lion of Oz, his tail between his legs, this man is timid. Perhaps he lacks self-confidence. He is fearful. He is hesitant. He needs courage to meet any kind of a danger. Easily frightened and fainthearted, he shies away from confrontational situations. He avoids dangers because his idea of self-preservation is not to take any risk and put himself in harm's way.

At the other end of that spectrum is *the daredevil.* The daredevil is audacious. He's hazardous and headstrong. He might well be reckless. Self-preservation doesn't seem to matter at all to him. He's willing to go headfirst into anything, often without thinking about any consequences.

The man on the self-preservation continuum really wants to be in balance. If you lean toward that cowardly side, you need to grasp the importance of courage to a man. It would be worthwhile to set goals that advance in difficulty and that contain some risk to your well-being. More importantly, you must consider what deeper issue is involved. Why are you unwilling to sacrifice self? Perhaps it's because of fear of death . . . or fear of failure. Could it be fear of intimacy? These are important battles for you to overcome to become more of the man God intended.

If you are more like the daredevil, you should ask God to give you a greater sensitivity to unwise decision making. You should also realize that this strength can be your "unguarded weakness," putting others in peril because of your sense of overconfidence. This behavior affects you more than you may realize as others may not be willing to trust you. Finding balance is important regardless of which side of the continuum you live.

Manhood Models

Perhaps no one knew of the future life waiting for him and so feared death less than a man named *Polycarp*, a celebrated figure in the history of Christianity. Polycarp was a pupil of the apostle John and lived between the years AD 70 and 155. His martyrdom is an astounding testimony to faith.

The emperors of Rome had unleashed bitter attacks against Christians during his lifetime. Members of the early church recorded many of their persecutions and deaths. Polycarp was arrested on the charge of being a Christian, a member of a politically dangerous cult whose rapid growth needed to be stopped. Amidst an angry mob, the Roman proconsul took pity on this gentle old man and simply said to him, "Proclaim Caesar is Lord." If Polycarp would only make this declaration and offer a small pinch of incense to Caesar's statue, he would escape torture and death.

To this Polycarp responded, "Eighty-six years I have served Christ, and he never did me any wrong. How can I blaspheme the King who saved me?"[4] Steadfast in his stand for Christ, Polycarp refused to compromise his beliefs and was burned at the stake. He knew heaven awaited.

Arland D. Williams appears to be a certain candidate for a manhood model. Air Florida Flight 90 had taken off from nearby Washington

National Airport during a steady snowstorm in 1982. Its wings had been deiced, but it waited and waited for clearance. When it finally took off, the jet's wings had begun icing again. The wing icing caused the aircraft to lose altitude and crash into a bridge, striking several cars before plunging into the Potomac River.

Of seventy-nine people on board, only six survived; one was Arland Williams. About age fifty, he was clinging to twisted wreckage, like the other survivors, bobbing in the icy Potomac. When the first helicopter arrived, the rescue team thought Williams seemed the most alert. They dropped life vests and then a floatation ball. But Williams promptly proceeded to pass those items along to other survivors.

> *"Greater love has no one than this, that he lay down his life for his friends."*
> ■ John 15:13

On two occasions, the crew recalled, he handed to someone else a lifeline that could have dragged him to safety. The helicopter crew rescued five people that day, two because of Williams' actions. Then the helicopter pilot Donald Usher returned to the scene to rescue that man who had passed the lifeline.

Arland Williams was nowhere to be found. He had sacrificed his life for others.

What would enable a man like that to decide to give his life for others? Arland D. Williams found a cause greater than himself that transcended self-preservation. Today, there is a bridge in Washington, D.C., named after this man.

Life and Freedom

A man who truly values life and freedom has a God-given passion. I hope you find life exhilarating. If you want to be alive and enjoy life, that is a godly passion. American men often undervalue the price of freedom. I hope you do not. It is a cause worth defending.

If you love life and freedom, you are a man with a great and noble passion.

Lasting freedom, of course, comes to those at peace in their souls. That's why followers of Jesus look for ways to be *life preservers*, seeking to rescue the lost and bring hope to all. The Bible describes these followers as "ambassadors" of the kingdom of God. We are the life preservers of this age. If you love Jesus, go out and throw a life preserver to someone with little hope.

Takeaways

For the man on the right kind of quest, I offer these nuggets to consider.

- *The importance of your life needs to be viewed on a grander scale, where forces of good and evil are vying for your soul.* An exceptional resource on developing your thinking in this area is the book *The Sacred Romance* by Brent Curtis and John Eldredge. I found my own heart challenged to see even daily activities playing out in a more important drama. You will see the significance that your life truly has. It is really worth reading.

- *The testing of your faith requires struggle.* No one else gets your set of challenges. Your problems are unique to you. *(Isn't that special???)* God knows the way you are wired because He did the wiring. (Read Psalm 139.) You will have your own course to manly maturity based on your personal design. There is no value in wishing you could be somebody else or have their situation. Be yourself and determine to ride the course that is yours and yours alone.

- *Emotional maturity is being able to handle and process the instability of life with adequate resources.* Everybody is going to have pain in life. Everybody is going to have stress. But not everybody will make the effort to establish safety nets to face these times. Circus performers use safety nets to keep from killing themselves in the event of a slip. Your safety nets are friends, family, counseling, reading materials, and insightful guides to help navigate through rough waters.

■ *Spiritual maturity involves a growing abandonment to self and focus on others.* The ultimate human instinct is self-preservation. Who wants not to live? This is where the deeper aspect of our soul enters in. As we find causes greater than ourselves, men can determine that while life is a beautiful and wonderful gift, there are higher purposes. Jesus gives us the clear example of self-sacrifice. He calls all men to develop this sense of the greater good with a growing abandonment of self and a focus on others.

■ *If you trust in Jesus, death is not your final answer.* It might be said that everybody wants eternal life (or the fountain of youth), but few are willing to grab it. God has given us the path. He has given us clear instruction. He has given us firm hope. Christians, in particular, should have extremely well developed hope meters because we have the ultimate hope . . . eternal life. When worries and hardships creep up, refuse to accept their nerve-wracking control. Remind yourself of God's abiding care and promise of eternal life!

Principles . . . of Self-Preservation

Here are a few key principles on self-preservation that I find important:

1. *God has provided all the resources required on this planet for human needs to be filled. We should be about* others' *preservation.* Resources are not scarce. We have a loving God who has provided abundantly. If there were enough men passionate about caring for others, our world would be very different. Millions

die each year from sheer neglect. That is not intended to provoke guilt. It is to challenge us all to think beyond ourselves and give others hope—the fuel of life.

2. *You cannot control outcomes, including your own passing. You can affect and direct your responses to outcomes.* Circumstances of life are beyond our control. We cannot control our destiny. I've read of a man who lived in Dallas and was considered a fitness model at one of the leading health centers in the country. He died a very young man quite unexpectedly. So a man needs to move beyond the cares of this world and direct his thoughts and actions to working for good in all circumstances without worrying of his image or reputation.

3. *Dying to self frees you from the bondage of self-preservation.* How does a man die to self? It is the conscious effort to look at his world from an "others perspective." A wise man can see what the best outcome looks like. In the process, if accomplishing those outcomes means he does not get all the credit or it costs him in the process, he will still pursue the right course. He is the man of destiny.

Notes

1. *California Star*, 13 February 1847; http://www.sfmuseum.org/hist6/donner.html.

2. "The Fateful Journey of the Donner Party," http://www.vics.edu/vwhansd/HIS121/Donner/html.

3. "'I Can't Hear Josh. I Can't Hear Josh': Parents Mourn Son Killed at Midway," *Chicago Sun Times*, 21 December 2005.

4. As quoted in Herbert Lockyer, *Last Words of Saints and Sinners* (Grand Rapids: Kregel, 1969), 152.

Insights on Self-Preservation

. . . with Erwin McManus

A lot of people deal with fear and pain. Even people who seem to be living courageous and joyful lives and who seem to be able to enjoy every single day face issues like fear and pain. The difference is that they're facing those issues differently.

Courage is not the absence of fear. Courage is the absence of self. It is the ability to live your life making decisions utilizing an internal compass based on the character of Christ and not on consequences or circumstances.

The first thing you have to do is to allow Jesus Christ to change you from the inside out. Find your own self-satisfaction, your sense of worth, meaning, and purpose, not in how your life is going but on how your character is forming.

A significant problem in contemporary Christianity is that many followers come to believe that just having knowledge that something is true or right should be enough to help. That really isn't so. We have enough people who believe in God, believe in Jesus, believe in Scriptures, who believe in the resurrection, who can barely make it through the day. And so, ironically—and it sounds almost sacrilegious to say this—believing in the resurrection doesn't necessarily give you a better day.

It's experiencing the *power of the resurrection* that changes us. The resurrection is the promise that there is no crisis, no obstacle, no problem, no circumstance that is greater than the power that Jesus Christ can give us to live each day.

Certain disciplines of the soul can help us overcome the difficulties of each day. I admit that I struggle hard with every discipline. And I think a lot of guys are like that. We look at men who are so disciplined and some seem naturally organized. Their whole world is ordered, and we make them our models or icons, and we can never live up to that.

The discipline that I try to make sure I never allow to falter is intimacy with God. I'll do whatever is necessary to make that happen, whether it's a significant time in the Scriptures, or time alone and praying, or walking and just blocking out the world, enjoying creation or nature. The discipline that we must form is connecting intimately with God, first and foremost, so that every day is lived in His presence. Then we won't look back on the day and go, "Oops! I forgot God."

When I experience deep personal loss—and I have had moments of incredible pain and hurt—I try to remember that the natural human instinct (because of our own brokenness and our own sinfulness) is to blame God for the problems. Instead of turning *from* God when I need Him most, I try to remember to turn *to* God when I need Him most.

During those times of pain, God wants us to cry out to Him and to be honest and transparent. The worst thing we can do in times of pain is to pretend to God that we're not hurting. A part of spiritual maturity is learning how to cry out to God and be strong for others. At the same time, we are to be neither fake nor pretentious. You and I need to be able to open up our hearts and let people see our pain and hurt. That's the power of the gospel, that even in our crying, there is joy. Even in our tears, there can be laughter; even in the darkest moment, there is always light.

The best way to fight fear is to stop thinking about the outcome of my choices and to think about the rightness of my choices. Yes, the right choice many times will bring you the most immediate pain and difficulty and conflict. We need to ask ourselves the question, "Am I willing, no matter how much fear I'm going to experience, and no matter how much pain I may be bringing to myself, to do that which is right and true and good?"

Finally, turn to your friends. Don't try to handle everything by yourself. Don't try to fix everything and then later share how God worked. Go to your closest friend and tell him, "Hey, I'm not doing well. I'm struggling; I need some help."

If you haven't developed meaningful friendships, recognize that this is where the church is so powerful. We try to pretend we can live a spiritual journey alone, but we cannot. We are created to take on this quest, this journey with others.

Erwin Raphael McManus is the lead pastor of Mosaic Church in Los Angeles. He is the catalyst behind Awaken, a collaboration of dreamers committed to creating environments that expand imagination and unleash creativity. Most of this material was extracted from his book Uprising: A Revolution of the Soul.

*Let us realize that the privilege
to work is a gift, that power to
work is a blessing, that love
of work is success.*

—David O. McKay

*Work hard and cheerfully at
whatever you do, as though
you were working for the Lord
rather than for people.*

—Colossians 3:23 (NLT)

7 The Passion for the Hunt

Since the creation, men have been the hunters and gatherers, the gardeners and the farmers. Some have been builders, artisans, skilled communicators, or thinkers. The Bible claims that men were given all these skills by God!

What the Bible doesn't say, however, is that God taught man to love his work more than anything else in life. But some men do. Finding balance in our attitudes toward "the hunt" is vital. Many of us are out of balance.

I've had my share of lousy jobs. One summer I worked at a retirement home in Montana, mainly mowing lawns and moving giant sprinkler pipes around. I hated that job. The pay could have tripled and I still would have hated it.

Later, I needed a job after taking a break from a year away at school and was hired at a new Radisson hotel in Minneapolis. As a houseman assigned to lots of cleanup tasks, ranging from cleaning windows and floors, bars, and elevators, to the disgusting job of applying some kind of toxic-smelling gel to the tile floors to clean them prior to the first use in a hotel room. Along with being on my knees a good part of the day, I'm not sure what I was inhaling but it was nasty stuff.

The best job I've ever had is what I do now. Before the sun rises, I drive forty miles to a Chicago radio station, do a half hour of final show prep, and then host a live radio program for four hours. Imagine . . . I get paid for giving things away to people, playing some good music, reading the newspaper, searching the Internet, and telling (sometimes) stupid jokes with my morning team and interviewing some very interesting people. What a country!

Another kind of work I love is developing organizations. Along with a couple of business ventures I have been involved in starting, I greatly enjoy creating strategies and systems to make a workplace function better. After taking several workstyle tests, it has become apparent that my work interests are in communication, organization, sales, and marketing. Conversely, I don't do well in mechanics, math, science, or anything that is too repetitive or has a lot of detail.

Is Your Job a Chore or an Addiction?

That's me. How about you? Do you find it hard to leave work every day because it is so stimulating and challenging? Or are you looking at the clock well before quitting time and waiting for the opportunity to get out? It has been my observation that most men live in one of those two worlds. Their work is a chore, or it is almost an addiction.

Men who have zero job satisfaction consider it only a way to get a paycheck. If they can somehow avoid doing the work, so much the better. There are attitudes—usually unhealthy ones—that correspond to this as it relates to the boss, the company, and the bottom line. Men who begrudge their work often begrudge all three of those as well. They can't wait for Friday so they can get out and have some *real* fun.

The addictive job is quite the opposite. The man will rise early and get into the office as fast as he can. He loves the thrill of using his skills (and sometimes his people) to make the most he can in life. The more success he has, the more it drives him. He will accept calls at night, at the ball game, and even on vacation. There is not enough time to get all his work done. His motto might well be, "Whatever It Takes." Unfortunately, it often takes more than he bargained for. Weekends, if not spent developing more business, are an interruption to the schedule. Sundays are often a day to "catch up"—on work that he couldn't do the rest of the week.

There is the middle ground, of course. These are the men who see their work as being a matter of necessity in life. They are moderately content in what they do but not overly committed to it. Finding a good job in a stable environment suits them fine. Good pay and benefits and low risk make life seem mostly worthwhile. Work is just something "you do."

Years ago work was mainly maintaining shelter and finding food—it was all about "the hunt." Today, if you are a hunter or a fisherman,

You can always find reasons to work. There will always be one more thing to do. But when people don't take time out, they stop being productive. They stop being happy.
■ Carisa Bianchi

Work for six days, and rest on the seventh. This will give your ox and your donkey a chance to rest. It will also allow the people of your household, including your slaves and visitors, to be refreshed.
■ Exodus 23:12 (NLT)

you clearly understand the hunt. While it is a wonderful thing to be out with other men or perhaps your son and create some bonding time, the real joy is making the catch. That's why you are there. It gives you a great sensation of success to know you've rounded up the next meal —even if you don't plan to eat it!

Bob Buford puts it well: "Pascal was right. Many of us do prefer the hunt to the capture. We find greater satisfaction from the thrill of the chase than from the successful completion of the conquest. Burying ourselves in the hustle and bustle of daily existence, we rarely take time out to experience the wonder and stillness of solitude, where the quiet voice of God is most audible."[1]

Gary Larson, the creator of the quirky, clever comic strip "The Far Side," is one of my favorite cartoonists. In fact, I recently received the complete two-volume, leather-bound set of his "Far Side" works. One of my favorites is a picture Gary drew of a dinosaur who is facing his daily appointment calendar. The dinosaur already checked off several days of activity . . . and each day is the same thing: Kill something and eat it!! He certainly had his work priorities in order!

Women just are not wired the same way as guys are when it comes to "the hunt." Yes, there are women who seem to enjoy going hunting or fishing. But a man's passion in this area stands apart from women. And most of the time, a man's passion for his work outshines his domestic interests—often beyond what is right.

How do you balance your attitude toward the hunt? We cannot deny this passion, which like all the others make a man . . . a man. Let's look at some of the components of the hunt.

Components of the Hunt

The Assignment

Our work life, aka the hunt, starts with knowing *the assignment.* The assignment is the acknowledgment that God has given man work to do as a blessing—but one that carries a curse. That's an interesting twist, isn't it?

God's original assignment for man's work was to tend the garden in which he was first placed. It says in Genesis 2:15: "The LORD God took the man and put him in the Garden of Eden to work it and take care of it." The Genesis account explains that because of the first man's disobedience, another dynamic in the work assignment resulted. In Genesis 3:17–19, we read, "Cursed is the ground because of you; through painful toil you will eat of it all the days of your life. It will produce thorns and thistles, and you will eat the plants of the field for you. By the sweat of your brow you will eat your food until you return to the ground, since from it you were taken; for dust you are to dust you will return."

That became the curse of man. Our work would include painful toil.

All men need to have work as a part of their life to fulfill God's intent for us. We are made to be *workers*. Recall, too, that God was the first worker. He's our role model. The Bible reveals that He worked six days on the expanse of creation. And then He rested.

The Provision

The second component is *the provision*. God has given every man what is needed to work in some capacity to serve others. He has provided the skills and talents needed to be productive. For example, Exodus 35:30–33 describes the skill of one gifted craftsman: "The LORD has chosen Bezalel son of Uri, the son of Hur, of the tribe of Judah, and he has filled him with the Spirit of God, with skill, ability and knowledge in all kinds of crafts—to make artistic designs for work in gold, silver and bronze, to cut and set stones, to work in wood to engage in all kinds of artistic craftsmanship." Who gave skill, knowledge, and special ability to man? This comes to us from our God. It is His provision.

We make a fundamental error believing we are the ones that are so smart, creative, and talented. Apart from Him, we could do nothing on our own.

The Calling

Our third component for the hunt is *the calling*, introduced in detail in an earlier chapter. Calling is the recognition that certain people have a unique sense of calling from God for a special purpose. But having a deep sense of calling is not necessary to fulfillment in the hunt. A man needs to feel *effective* in what he does, and the more he connects his work with a higher purpose (i.e., serving others), the more likely his need for a sense of accomplishment will be met.

Furthermore, the Western business approach frequently gives a mistaken impression to workers that if they do not rise to management, they haven't achieved success. But each of us has distinct gifts. We cannot all do the same tasks well. In certain tasks, though, we will excel.

In *The E Myth*, Michael Gerber analyzes why many entrepreneurs fail. He separates the needs of an organization into visionary work, management skills, and the actual labor needed to make a successful business. Usually, an entrepreneur starts an enterprise with the idea that he can be all of those things. Or maybe he doesn't recognize that he needs all of those components for his business. Inevitably, the failings to be effective at all three areas will result in some failure within the business.

This explains, in part, why entrepreneurs so often fail. Rare is the breed of man who brings all three kinds of skills to the table. Why? Because God has wired us specifically with certain gifts. It's the beauty of His arrangement. It is important to recognize the value of the contributions of others.

The Mastery

Next in our components is *the mastery*—the pursuit of excellence. This is expected of man in his area of work. Yes, God truly has entrusted you with specific gifts and skills. However, the mastery of those talents is your challenge in life. As you pursue excellence in your work, you demonstrate an honor for God and for His kingdom. Excellence involves the *quality* of the work, the *attitude* by which it is done, the *intent* by which that work is performed—whether it's purely for self-ish motivation or for others—and the *legitimacy* of the work.

That last work, *legitimacy*, deserves some explanation. Our best efforts as men come when we provide a useful product or service for our fellow man. When we engage in an unworthy endeavor, such as running a casino or promoting illicit or immoral behavior, we are not about a legitimate work as would be viewed by God. We are hurting our fellow man rather than helping. While those who engage in this may approach their work with a certain quality, they miss the mark in excellence because of legitimacy.

Keeping Perspective

Our final component in the hunt is *the challenge of keeping perspective.* I am encouraging you as a man to maintain a steady attitude like that of Jesus Christ in whatever kind of work you do. This is most clearly accomplished when you focus on meeting the needs of others. Mission and purpose statements that create organizations for profit miss the point completely. That is a potential win-lose venture. You could win, and it's OK if someone else loses. That is not the way of Jesus. Going to work each day out of strictly selfish motivation leaves man unsatisfied. We must not lose sight of the spiritual meaning of work.

This is the connecting point that we have to God in our work. It defines a critical role in life we play, regardless of the kind of work we do. A man who meets the challenge never loses sight of the spiritual purpose of his work.

A man's passion for the hunt is among the most time-consuming of his passions and therefore also may be the most difficult to manage. Why did God design man with this desire to work? It is because it is *His nature to work*, and we are made in His image.

The Hunt Continuum

The continuum of the hunt will help a man examine his heart toward work. At the far left is *the man of sloth*. He has an aversion to work or exertion. He is lazy. But sloth has a second definition. The quality of this man's work may lack any semblance of true excellence. Sloth not only means that we are not working hard or that we're not working at all. It can also mean that we're just doing a lousy job of it. That's the man of sloth. Even loitering excessively can describe a man of sloth.

At the other end of the continuum is the man focused on perfection in the hunt. *The perfectionist* makes the workplace unbearable for another reason. He is virtually impossible to please. You can never quite do enough for this guy. He is demanding, unyielding, and often intemperate when people slip up. He is exact, nitpicky, almost microscopic in his quest to get things just right. A perfectionist will commit himself to an extreme set of work demands and put those same demands on others. Typically, the perfectionist wants everyone to meet his expectations and be consumed with that effort because *work and achievement is the total meaning of this person's life.*

The Hunt Continuum

The Man of Sloth   **The Perfectionist**

In Balance

If you're at either extreme, how do you get in balance? For the man of sloth, he needs a wake-up call: If he believes the old phrase "good enough for government work," he has a slothful heart. The lazy man or the man inattentive to important details is disrespecting his manhood.

Conversely, the perfectionist has created a world that no one can meet. We are all going to make mistakes. Not everything is as important as the perfectionist makes it out to be. The man who works diligently to offer his best and pursue excellence while keeping the idea of work as simply one aspect of life will be in the best position to enjoy both his work and his life.

Manhood Models

Sam Minor is not a household name. I met Sam when I lived in Pittsburgh in the 1990s. Sam was a champion wrestler for Penn State, a Big Ten conference champion. He had a real interest in farming, but after he got his degree from Penn State, he went to work for a breeding company. It was certainly an "OK job," but he missed the farm life. It was a natural thing for him. Later Sam went to California and worked for the Carnation Company. He was only there a year and decided to return to the life he loved. So he moved his family back to the western Pennsylvania area and they looked for some farm property.

The property Sam wanted needed to meet one very important criterion: the traffic count that came past the farm. Sam knew that a small dairy farm could not make it on its own. So he built a restaurant on the property as well, called the Spring House. It was all part of the plan from day one. You'll find it today in a town called Eighty Four, Pennsylvania, which is the home of 84 Lumber. The Spring House will prepare you the most wonderful home-cooked meal.

All the family members have worked at the restaurant. It is the most charming, delightful place. Sam pitches in too, whenever he has breaks from his dairy farming.

> *Every job is a self-portrait of the person who does it. Autograph your work with excellence.*
> ■ Unknown

Sam Minor, when I knew him, was still getting up at three or four in morning taking care of his dairy cows. And on those hot summer nights you could find Sam at eight o'clock taking care of his dairy cows, sweating all the while. But he just loves what he does.

S. Truett Cathy, the founder and the chairman of the Chick-fil-A, also has found balance in the hunt. Truett entered the restaurant business back in 1946 with a little place called the Dwarf Grill. In 1967, he opened up his first Chick-fil-A restaurant in Atlanta. Today, more than a thousand Chick-fil-A's dominate the southeastern United States, although franchises are as far west as California. Truett Cathy is a deeply spiritual man who has built his life and his business on hard work and biblical principles.

Chick-fil-A stores are not open on Sunday, because Cathy believes that a man needs to have a day off for family to rest. The company offers a wonderful scholarship program to help their employees. The firm has a reputation for treating people fairly. Their commercials remain among the most creative in the fast-food business, with those cows telling us all to "eat more chiken" (yes, it's spelled *chiken*) and go light on their beef brethren.

The company's official statement of purpose declares that Chick-fil-A seeks "to glorify God by being a faithful steward of all that is entrusted to us and to have a positive influence on all who come in contact with Chick-fil-A." That belief results in scholarship programs, character-building programs for kids, foster homes, and other community services. Each year the company raises thousands of dollars for charities and scholarships as the official sponsor of college football's Peach Bowl.[2]

Do You Love or Hate Your Work?

The nature of work is something that men often hate or something they love. The more natural the work is to you, the more you will tend to love it. But remember, your work is most satisfying when you serve others. It will give you great peace as well. A man who sets his limits on what work is—and is not—is a wise man.

As you desire to have the mind of Christ, your desire will focus on finding kingdom value through your work. Seek to honor the kingdom and serve others through your work, and at the final bell, you can expect to hear those words from the Lord, "Well done, good and faithful servant!"

Takeaways

For a man pursuing a life worth living, consider these perspectives on the hunt:

- *You have been equipped; you have been gifted to serve mankind with your work.* Knowing this should alter our perspective on our work. What a privilege to know that among all of God's creation, you have unique and creative abilities that serve a higher purpose. We greatly undervalue what our Creator has endowed us with. Once you realize and act upon those gifts, you have tremendous potential to make a difference in this world.

- *All work done properly is done to improve the quality of life for others.* What is it that drives inventors? Almost all innovation comes from the desire to improve some condition of life. Do you give time to considering how your work is truly making life better for others? If not, make that a priority. It should cause you to rise above mediocrity in all you do.

- *A man's work brings him honor and is a vital component to his self-esteem.* This should not be underestimated. Talk to a man who has been unemployed for a lengthy period and you will know what a terrible thing it can be to a man's self-esteem. On the other hand, a man takes personal pride in becoming skilled in his line of work, which also gives him a sense of honor internally and external praise.

- *Diligence in any kind of good labor honors God.* Diligence takes form in a conscientious, hardworking approach to the primary duties of the job. It is easy to allow ourselves to engage in activities at work which are not of significance or part of our assignment. That ranges from doing tasks we enjoy rather than those which yield the most productivity to engaging in items of personal business while on the job. Furthermore, it covers the lack of attention to detail which results in sloth. Diligent effort—being paid for what we do and do well—honors God.

■ *We must do whatever we can to help a brother unemployed, or one who has lost his job, regardless of the circumstances.* As noted above, a man's work plays into his self-esteem. With our busy lives, it is easy for us to "feel badly" about someone else's misfortune, but not to do anything about it. The minimum we can do is to let someone unemployed know we care. We can pray for that person. We might suggest a job lead or a contact to make. Knowing someone cares about your situation when you are hurting can really boost the hope factor.

■ *Attitude truly does change the nature and the quality of the work being performed.* Much has been said on this topic by motivational speakers. It's all true. Attitude impacts the worker along with everyone he comes in contact with. You can tell when a man enjoys his work. You can tell the opposite as well. The Bible teaches that a man should work as if he is working for God, and not for men (see Colossians 3:23). With that in mind, we owe it to all parties to "get in the game" with our attitude.

Principles . . . of the Hunt

Here are a few principles of the passion for the hunt:

1. *A man must not love his work more than his God, his family, or his own well-being.* If a man's achievement leaves a trail of broken relationships, the price is too high. If you enjoy your

work, ensure that you have checkpoints built into your life to guard against the false god of job success.

2. *A man honors God by using integrity regarding company time, materials, and coworkers.* There are many ways a man can sacrifice integrity in his work. He can be an abuser of his time. He can take company resources for personal use. He can ask coworkers to be his personal stewards. The man of integrity observes boundaries in all areas of the job.

3. *A man's work performance is enhanced by proper rest, as God instructed.* Take whatever vacation you earn. Especially set aside one day a week. I am always surprised to hear of men who have not taken vacation during a year. For some it's even longer. It may seem like the company cannot do without you. Trust me; it can. Vacations give you renewed perspective. A day off a week will add to your productivity. Take the time allotted to you.

Notes

1. Bob Buford, *Halftime* (Grand Rapids: Zondervan, 1994), 64.

2. The 2005 Chick-fil-A Peach Bowl raised more than $500,000 for charities and scholarship programs. See http://www.chick-fil-a.com/PeachBowlSponsor.asp.

Insights on the Hunt
. . . with Bill Hendricks

God cares deeply about everyday work. This truth actually goes contrary to many people's understanding that work is a curse. If you look at the biblical account in Genesis, you discover that work was given to us *before* the curse. In fact, it was given to us as a gift, and something that God assigned to us, not with a sense of labor and toil. That's really what the curse introduced, but with a sense of serving God as His steward over the creation. The curse introduced fallenness of the world—sin—and so that makes the world less cooperative. But it doesn't diminish the dignity of work.

Every single human being is endowed to do specific kinds of work. God has gifted every man. Ephesians 2:10, for example, says that we're God's workmanship, His made thing, His crafted thing, like a tool or an implement that is specifically designed to do a good work as unto the Lord.

Whatever your gift, God values it. Every society values certain kinds of work differently than others. Imagine if we all lived in a society that valued the hunting and gathering of food: The fast guys and the guys who had really great eyeballs would be prized greatly because they could hunt really well. But we must not lose sight of the fact that all of our work really does matter to God. We might rank certain things, but in God's economy, He sees a place and a value for each of us.

I realize that at some point a man may find himself unemployed, and he really wants to find work. Unemployment is, to some degree, a result of the fall that influences how economies function. The national economy and the circumstances of the economy may not cooperate with one's personal aspirations and a man must understand that.

Unemployment is a great time to build one's character. It also is a great time to build one's faith. Just because you don't have a job, and you're struggling to find a job, who says God isn't working to provide you with a job? I could tell you many stories of men who, after praying and praying, didn't seem to be able to find a job. Then after they found the job, they discovered that all kinds of forces were at play all the time they were praying. What we're called to in those very difficult times is both faith and diligence to be out actively and aggressively doing what we can from our side to find that job.

Finally, don't assume that constant promotion and climbing "the ladder of success" is the goal. Actually, not everybody is motivated to move up a ladder. Some people are, and they assume that everybody else ought to be, and they may even encourage others, such as their kids, to aspire to that. Look at your giftedness and learn where you excel.

Many people have no aspiration to be the person in charge or at the top of the ladder. That's actually one of the problems with promotions. We assume that higher up the ladder is better, and we often promote people into work that really doesn't fit them. That becomes a problem. My challenge both to individuals, as well as to employers, is find out what the person does best, put them in that, and wherever it is in the food chain as it were, remunerate fairly and accordingly. And then, let them do their work.

Bill Hendricks directs The Giftedness Center in Dallas, created to help individuals with job fit, career development, executive coaching, and midlife guidance. He is author or coauthor of several books, including Your Work Matters to God.

In our amusements a certain limit is to be placed that we may not devote ourselves to a life of pleasure and thence fall into immorality.

—Marcus Tullius Cicero

Godliness with contentment is great gain.

—1 Timothy 6:6

8 The Passion of Pleasure

Growing up, I found pleasure in many things. Building forts, snowball fights, and after-school games were delights waiting for us after those long days at school. I loved running through the outfield at top speed and catching a long fly ball. And I really loved going to Minnesota Twins games in the summer, eating ballpark dogs, and cheering for the hometown heroes. That was pure pleasure.

During the sixth grade I discovered another kind of pleasure—that was when I first saw one of the "men's magazines." Sometimes during the mile walk home after school with a couple of friends, we would stop at a drugstore where they had a magazine rack. As cleverly and discreetly as possible, we found ways to gaze at those forbidden pages of *Playboy* and discover a new kind of "pleasure."

While I didn't fully understand the nature of this pleasure, it was very captivating. Eventually, the drugstore manager would catch on and shoo us away, but the seeds had been planted. It wouldn't be long before sex was what guys were always talking about in junior high and senior high.

I open this chapter on pleasure with that story since a man's sexual drive is normally the strongest of his pleasure drives. I've been told that certain drugs can generate feelings that exceed the sensation of rapture generated by sex but I have no experience there. But I do know that a man's sex drive is very potent. As the song says, "It can drive a strong man to his knees." Many a man have found their knees weak in the presence of a woman they find irresistible.

When does this intense drive finally subside? One seventy-five-year-old fellow was asked that question and he said, "I don't know, but it must be after seventy-five." Because sexual pleasure brings us a sense of escape and is intensely satisfying, it is hard to resist. For some men, it becomes their downfall.

Pleasure is a critical passion for us to understand because it can become our greatest weakness. It can keep us spiritually handicapped. It can open the door for our downfall, including our reputation. It can ruin us on every front: physically, emotionally, mentally, and spiritually. It brings us dead center with the word "sin."

Our Deepest Longings

What exactly is the passion of pleasure? It is the satisfying of our *deepest longings.* These longings come to us on two very specific planes. The Bible teaches us that we have two natures and one of them is the *natural man.* This is the one that all men are the most familiar with. Other terms we might use would be the *carnal man,* or the *flesh.* Those are terms the Bible uses most frequently to describe these urgings that a man has, these passions that we pursue as pleasure. They are the ways man finds to satisfy his fleshly urgings. That's the carnal man. Some of these are safe . . . like our love for sports. Hobbies give us pleasure. (Playing golf supposedly does but I'm not sure my rounds have given me much pleasure.) The flesh-minded, earthly, carnal, natural man seeks out things that give him pleasure.

But the Bible describes another dimension common to every one of us. It's called the *spiritual man.* The spiritual man has a soul, a spirit, an inner self that ultimately defines who he is and what his character is about. If you are a follower of Christ and have put your hope and your trust in Him, something very special has happened in your life. A supernatural transformation has occurred that gives you a power beyond yourself to deal with the seemingly overwhelming influences on your natural man.

Just as the flesh craves to be satisfied, the spirit longs for pleasure in many ways as well. Ultimately, the soul yearns for peace.

Even people who haven't had a soul transformation have a spiritual core to them. It's just not activated. The Bible says this condition is a man who is spiritually dead. Another way to look at this is like being "plugged in" to a power source. The cord with the connector is ready to go, but until it is plugged in, there is no flow of electricity and thus, no power.

When our spiritual man becomes activated, he finds there is great pleasure to be found in ways he did not know before. That pleasure comes from the serving of others and meeting the needs of others. It creates a deep satisfaction. There is an actual term for it: *joy*! This is a state of being in which men come to realize that there is more to life than the carnal man, more to life than satisfying the pleasure drives of the carnal man.

Let me get more specific in sorting out these two very different states of man. What are the things in life that give the natural man the most pleasure? What are things that give *you* the most pleasure in the flesh as a human being? Again, sex is pretty much at the top of the list for most guys. I know this to be true because I have worked with men long enough to hear the stories. Beyond that, I have had access to research information that reveals how often a man thinks about sex. In one survey from the group Promise Keepers, about 65 percent of the men said they were dealing with pornography issues. It is the number one point of pleasure that puts a man at risk in relationships.

Pleasure Places

There are other flesh-satisfying pleasures, of course. For example, food. Men know that food is a need for survival. But the pleasure of food goes well beyond that. Advertisers know that they can get a man to salivate with a picture of a big, juicy steak. Or pizza. Or pancakes, bacon, and eggs. Some men eat to live. But many men live to eat.

Another pleasure place for men is achievement. Watch a football game and some of the more incredible and sometimes bizarre end-zone celebrations after a touchdown and you'll know this is true. When a man accomplishes something, there is a feeling of exhilaration. Pleasure.

As noted, carnal pleasures can consume a man. For the purposes of our discussion, I would categorize the carnal pleasures this way: sex, drugs, rock 'n' roll. I don't know who coined that phrase, but it defines us pretty well. Another has said a man's loves are "wine, women, and song." You get the picture. These are big pleasure places many men are tempted to visit.

> *Many a man thinks he is buying pleasure, when he is really selling himself to it.*
> ■ Benjamin Franklin

Because of our preoccupation with sex, I rank that at the top of a man's pleasure drive. But drugs are also big pleasures. By *drugs* I mean all addictions of life aside from sex. Those addictions are many—food, money, fame—and of course, drugs. Anything that holds physical or emotional power over you is an addiction.

"Rock 'n' roll" can be defined as *the party life*. At one Super Bowl halftime show, the performer screamed to the crowd, "Come on, Houston; let's party!!!!" That defines it pretty well. Most men love to party. Of course, the party life can be tame and relatively safe, or it can be wild and sensually overwhelming. The party is a carnal man's way of going out and having fun and focusing on pleasure.

Please note that I am not being critical of the passion for pleasure. A man is wired this way—to enjoy life! It is when the pursuit of pleasure controls a man that harm occurs. For the spiritual man, who still has two natures, this leads to conflict between the two. (Paul describes well the conflict between those natures and the tendency toward sin in Romans 7.) Uncontrolled, the carnal pleasures can quickly stunt a man's spiritual growth.

God's Plan Regarding Pleasure

As you now know, this book is written to help you achieve balance in the passions of your life as a man. At the creation of Earth and all living things, God gave to man a desire for pleasure. We are made in God's image. Many things give God pleasure. He wanted man to enjoy pleasure as well. Adam was able to walk around the garden and go, "Wow! Does that ever look good! Man, does *this* taste good!" And, of course, God created Eve and she was pleasing to man. Oh, yeah.

But He also formed that first man as a spiritual man at the time of creation. That was to keep him in balance. Adam's spiritual condition was in sync with God. That balance was disturbed in the garden of Eden when Adam chose a different course. He experienced spiritual death when his relationship with God was broken and needed reconciliation. That is our situation. We follow Adam in our spiritually broken state from birth. We need reconciliation. We have that available through faith in Jesus Christ. If we don't reconcile with God, we live apart from Him, knowing only the passions for pleasure and spending our days seeking to satisfy them.

Components of Pleasure

Biological Response

The components of the pleasure passion begin with the *biological response.* What makes pleasure pleasurable are the chemical changes, the emotions, the feelings, and sensations created by satisfying a human desire. When I say you are wired to enjoy pleasure, it is obvious your physical response proves it! God put all the right things inside of your human body so that you could enjoy a pleasurable experience.

Pleasure feels good to you for a reason. It is supposed to. Intense pleasure is meant to feel intensely good. Let me clarify that pleasure is not sin. Again, you were wired to enjoy things in life, to find things of pleasure. In the carnal man, you will always long for things that satisfy the flesh. When pleasure is kept in balance and in check by applying boundaries, you will find the legitimate enjoyment in pleasure. But if it's out of balance, eventually pleasure will become unsatisfying, and you will demand more and extreme pleasures.

Pleasure, however, should not be confused with joy. Joy is a condition we train ourselves to live in regardless of circumstances.

Satisfaction Quotient

Next is the *satisfaction quotient.* By that I mean the amount of activity in terms of frequency or intensity by which this pleasure is met. Pleasure is to be part of life, not our mission or our pursuit. If you find yourself craving pleasure to keep yourself happy, there's likely to be an imbalance. If you have to have pleasure to remain motivated in life, it's out of balance.

People wanting an escape from pain or other trials often escape into excess pleasure. During times of stress or great difficulties, a man's escape mechanism is frequently pleasure devices that are out of bounds. He seeks something to offset that which he feels is holding him back.

But the pleasure can never satisfy. In fact, it will demand more and more of you to achieve the escape, the "high." Drug abusers know that it takes more and more "junk" to keep a high going. So it is with the pursuit of pleasure. Using artificial means to achieve pleasure will require more each time to keep you satisfied. Count on it.

Contrasts

The third component in pleasure is *contrasts*, the differences in the way that pleasure is achieved and perceived. What are some of those contrasts?

■ *Biological versus emotional.*

■ *Pleasing self instead of deriving pleasure from pleasing others.*
Once the carnal man becomes the spiritual man, he will notice
a contrast in his life of how he finds pleasure in making a difference in the lives of others.

■ *Temporal versus eternal.* We can see that a view of the long term
instead of the short term generates a more sustaining pleasure.

■ *Natural versus the artificial.* Talk show host Rush Limbaugh
has had to battle with an addiction to painkillers. Starting off
as a medical necessity, this synthetic painkiller became necessary to keep his pleasure need satisfied. Chemicals are not a
natural way to find happiness or satisfaction in life.

■ *Things in bounds and things out of bounds.* Simply stated, a
man has to know his limitations on pleasure and have clear
boundaries about what is permissible. Alcohol usage would be
a good example here. Good judgment is required.

Consequences

The fourth component of pleasure is *consequence*. The consequences of the pleasure passion measure the impact on our lives which
the pursuit of pleasure creates. In balance, pleasure delivers spice to life
and is one of the wonderful rewards of the human experience. I believe men are more prone than women to seek fun at the expense of
family and work. Men foolishly accept the consequences of their pursuit of pleasure at great cost.

Each man must ask, "Does my involvement in seeking pleasure create any harm to others?" That could be anything from an addiction
to golf, to your work, to something artificial, or to the desires for sexual stimulation. If these pursuits limit your ability to function in a
healthy way, you have to get control.

Using pleasure to avoid reality only delays the consequences of our being unable to cope. Eventually a man has to deal with those consequences. When pleasure becomes our God, it keeps us from the true God.

Why Pleasure?

All four components apply to every man's pleasure passion. Pleasure is among the most instinctive and at the same time, potentially destructive of his passions. It may be the most difficult one to lay aside. So why did God create man with the desire for pleasure? Because God wants men to have an abundant life. He loves the idea that we find pleasure in the things that He has created for us.

God wants us to celebrate life—but always within His design.

The Pleasure Continuum

The pleasure continuum is unique in that it defines our state of being. On one side, we find *pain and depression.* This is the man who has no pleasure in life. In this state, a man cannot find any activity that seems to produce sufficient joy, any stimulus that has consistency which can bring him happiness in life. He is basically an unsatisfied and an unfulfilled soul.

When there is excessive pain and depression, and it could be either one or both, the normal functions that bring about pleasure are inhibited. A man may then turn to unhealthy use of drugs or other stimuli to give him a pleasure buzz. This man may also border on being suicidal. He just cannot find happiness.

The Pleasure Continuum

Pain and Depression   **Constant Euphoria**

In Balance

Being out of balance in this way is usually obvious. You are simply *not* enjoying life. You cannot seem to enjoy what others find so naturally enjoyable—family, work, friends, and generally happy experiences. If this is you, then counseling might be well advised. There is a difference between psychological or psychiatric help and counseling. Extreme cases may require some kind of chemical or in-patient treatment.

Frequently, though, a man may simply need another wise person to help him sort out his pain and depression issues. You could start with a trusted friend and get his input. If you cannot find satisfaction, consider getting some professional help.

At the other end of our continuum is *constant euphoria.* For this man, life must be a series of highs. If it doesn't produce pleasure, he moves on to what will in life. This man is always looking to make himself happy. All the energy he musters is to bring pleasure to himself. If you find yourself edging to this side of the continuum, your life will be marked with visible signs. Each day you will look for ways to satisfy cravings. You may find it difficult to delay gratification or to sacrifice your longings for pleasure. This is not going to get better.

Your best solution is to admit it—and find a few friends who can be your support group. Your spouse may need to be involved. Addictions are hard to admit for a man. It suggests we are weak and not in control. There is a reason for that. It is because often we *are* weak and not in control! That's what it means to be human!

A dramatic example of a person who carries both extremes is the manic-depressive. A former college quarterback told me his manic depression cost him dearly in marriages and other aspects of his life. When on the "high end," he became extremely creative and productive and could hardly sleep. It was like a steady high. Then he would "crash" and find it very difficult to function. This is an example of a treatable problem that may require chemical assistance.

You and I are somewhere along this key continuum. We may be living more in pain and depression or moving toward more self-gratification. To be real men, we need to be balanced. We want to experience pain as it is meant to be—a real part of life. And we want to experience pleasure in its fullness but within boundaries. We are then able to live our lives in a state of joy, a condition possible for the human soul.

Manhood Models

For *"Bill W."* the pleasure passion—and thus his life—was out of balance because of alcohol. Drinking was the focus of his life; he admitted the imbalance and sought help through others and God. Bill became one of the cofounders, along with Sam Schumaker, of Alcoholics Anonymous (AA).

In the beginning of AA, a newcomer to the meetings had to identify that he was "licked with the problem and he would do whatever it took to get fixed." These men would spend time meeting with a medical person who would explain the disease of alcoholism, the best that they understood it. Each man was then asked two questions: Do you believe in God? Are you willing to get down on your knees and pray? The newcomer was then asked to give his life to Jesus Christ as Lord and Savior.

> *He who loves pleasure will become poor; whoever loves wine and oil will never be rich.*
> ■ Proverbs 21:17

Over time, AA softened some of the language. Today they use the term "higher power" in place of God. The group is known by its powerful "Twelve Steps program."[1] The best part about AA? It forces a man to admit he is out of control and needs help.

In the men's ministry work I have done over the years, it is fundamental that we encourage men to become involved in a small group. It is there a man can build relationships with a few trusted friends. Hopefully he can admit he is simply a pilgrim on the journey of life, struggling in the ordinary details of life.

Fred Stoeker attended Stanford University and was what many would call a "cool guy." But he is brutally honest about his sexual history, revealed in *Every Man's Battle: Winning the War on Sexual Temptation One Victory at a Time*. He writes that the first time he had sex with a girl, it was the girl he was sure he wanted to marry. The next time, it was with somebody he hoped he'd marry. Then it was with somebody he thought he might marry. After that, he didn't care whether he married the girl or not. But God had a plan for Fred's life and he came to follow Jesus. And he met Brenda and they got married.

Fred threw himself into his sales career and his family. His world seemed fine. But his mind was far from pure. There was fantasy thinking and viewing things he knew he shouldn't. Fred wrote:

> *I continued feeling distant from God. . . . My prayer life was feeble. Once my son was very sick and had to be rushed to the emergency room. Did I rush into prayer? No. I could only rush to ask others to pray for me. . . . I had no faith in my own prayers, because of my sin. . . . My faith was weak in other ways as well. . . . I had no peace. . . . I was paying a price for my sin.*[2]

Fred admits that his marriage suffered as well. He couldn't commit 100 percent to Brenda, out of fear that she might dump him later. He adds, "At church I was an empty suit. I never arrived ready to minister to others. Of course, my prayers were no more effective in God's house than anywhere else. My church was paying a price." The relationships with his children were also suffering.

Finally, Fred made the connection between his sexual immorality and his distance from God. His story is one of the most powerful and memorable a man can read.

Pleasure and the Homosexual Lifestyle

I must address one more area of sexual temptation some men face: homosexuality. The estimated number of men involved in the homosexual lifestyle range from 6 to 10 percent. I don't know what percentage is the most accurate, and I'm not sure that it really matters. Homosexuality has become a divisive issue in the church, which is unfortunate, because the Bible is quite clear on the subject —practicing homosexual sex is sin. It must be discouraged and men who are tempted in this way must view this as any other temptation which is beyond the boundaries set by God.

Having said this, let me address the issue for those who struggle with homosexual temptation. All men have a sin nature, what we identified earlier in this chapter as the *natural man*. With this sin nature you may have found that you are attracted to other men. I don't know why that is, but significantly, it may feel like you can't change. You might even ask, "Why should I?"

Fred Stoeker might have asked the same question—not about homosexuality, but about why he should give up pursuing sexual relationships with women *on his terms*. But Fred knew why he had to quit. He knew what the boundaries were. He knew that from reading the Bible.

In the same way, deep down you may know what the boundaries are as well. You may find it extremely difficult to live within those boundaries, which means giving up the homosexual lifestyle. Or you may have to fight the temptation on a daily basis. But it is a battle worth fighting to keep your heart as a man.

There is a secondary message here. For those men who do not struggle with homosexual interests and feel uneasy toward men in the homosexual lifestyle, recognize any barrier you put up toward another man who is tempted in this way. Your barrier could inhibit his healing. In the church, we have work to do, both teaching the truth about homosexuality and loving all men so that those tempted in this way feel accepted as men. It is very difficult to find healing when you can't find any support or understanding. All of us need a support system. The church is created to be that support system.

Taking the Right Pleasure Path

Pleasure is a wonderful thing that God's given to you. It is also the road to pain and problems if left unattended. It's up to you to decide which path to take. Remember, a man who can set his boundaries on pleasure, and who has a means of self-examination with accountability is well-prepared to stay on the right path and resist temptations to go the selfish route.

You can win the battle—and make no mistake, there is a battle we must face in guarding our hearts. It is an individual battle. Don't go it alone.

A man who truly knows how to enjoy life with pleasure—and within boundaries—has a God-given passion. God intended for you to enjoy life. He created pleasure for you!

Takeaways

For the man on the right kind of quest, pleasure is a God-given part of life. Here are some guidelines in using this gift from God.

- *Pleasure gives us relief from stress and contributes to our emotional balance.* What a wonderful gift from God to experience pleasure! Enjoy it. And recognize that the presence of pleasure has benefits for your health as well as the enjoyment it provides.

- *Because pleasure yields varying degrees of euphoric response, a man can easily become trapped by the enticement of this passion.* Pleasure ought to come with a warning label: "Watch out! This could be hazardous!" Depending on pleasure for contentment is the danger sign.

- *If the pursuit of pleasure becomes a primary drive or focus in our life, and it goes unchecked, we are out of balance and become callous to our priorities and to human needs around us.* This statement is made after observing a number of men who put fun and games ahead of family priorities. It can also be said these same activities can be used to avoid interaction with God.

■ *Because our carnal nature rejects limits put on our lives, we must choose the way of discipline and say no to excess pleasure.* It is true. Our carnal nature rejects limits. Americans define themselves as a free people. To many, that implies freedom from anyone putting limits on their lives. That is perceived as liberty, but it is treated as license. A wise man learns the difference between liberty and license. According to America's founding documents, liberty means people are called to be "self-governing," so that democracy may survive.

■ *A man's best defense against the abuse of pleasure is a good offense. Your best offense is an accountability plan.* Find a few trusted friends to help you stay within the boundaries of pleasure. But it is you who must be proactive in making that happen. You are the only one who will allow someone else to have access to your life.

■ *Giving others pleasure within boundaries intensifies our own level of joy and deep satisfaction.* It is an ironic but true statement. That is how God's economy works: Lose to win. Give to gain. Die to live. When it comes to pleasure, we find something similar working. As we seek to give others pleasure, we find our own quotient of happiness increased.

Principles . . . of Pleasure

Here are two key principles of pleasure I believe will help you:

1. *The man who has the Spirit of God in his heart denies himself certain pleasure to avoid becoming spiritually weak and to reveal God's power.* The spiritually mature man has recognized that God's limits are there for a purpose. Living within those limits

will give him spiritual confidence of God's power and added strength.

2. *The path to freedom from the tyranny of temptation is possible one victory at a time.* Followers of Jesus are to consider themselves dead to sin. You may see your battle as one you cannot win. But that is not the case. The road may be difficult, and the battle must be fought one step at a time. If you have put your faith in Jesus, then you must embrace the truth that the Holy Spirit has come to live inside of you, offering a kind of power that is truly life changing. But God does not force these heart changes upon you. He calls on us to submit willingly to His greater purposes.

Notes

1. Step two reads: "We came to believe that a Power greater than ourselves could restore us to sanity." Step three reads: "We made a decision to turn our will and our lives over to the care of God as we understood him."

2. Steve Arterburn and Fred Stoeker, with Mike Yorkey, *Every Man's Battle* (Colorado Springs: WaterBrook, 2000), 18.

Insights on Pleasure
. . . *with Steve Arterburn*

One of my early passions for pleasure manifested itself in my ending about sixty pounds heavier than I am today. I loved food and ate it anytime I could get ahold of it. And in the worst forms! I was fascinated by Sarah Lee and Miss Debbie and would have been a lover to either of them!

There was another pleasure that I pursued and had a passion for: I was a very promiscuous guy. It was really a result of me being a very disconnected person. My life was not connected to people relationally, and I was living kind of a dead existence—doing a lot of things but needing always something just to make me feel alive.

On our radio program, *New Life Live*, the most common problem I'm hearing about is either a person or a marriage being destroyed because of Internet pornography. That is the biggest area that every man needs to be aware of and to get it under control by surrendering that to God. Of course, all forms of pornography are equally dangerous. It's very tough to go to a newsstand without seeing a lot of sexually explicit images. A man really has to make a decision about what he is going to fill his mind with. If he doesn't have a plan of attack, he's going to stumble.

I think many times men fear becoming truly intimate. They don't want to pay the price of developing a serious relationship, or they're afraid of being judged in a truly sexually intimate relationship. A lot men really question their manhood. They do things just to try to establish that they are a man.

I believe that manhood is expressed in an intimate relationship with a woman where she provides all of the sexual gratification that he would experience, where she is approving of various forms of sexual gratification, and is involved in all of those ways. When a man is involved sexually with a woman in that way, that's where he can express himself and his manhood and truly experience what God wants him to experience as a man. We settle for the counterfeits and the cheap substitutes and we really miss what God intended for us as men.

When a man turns to pornography, he replaces intimacy with intensity. He replaces the ongoing development of a relationship with instant gratification. But it's interesting what pornography has done to men. Pornography hasn't made men more sexual and turned them on more and brought them closer to women. It has actually neutered them. You see men no longer wanting to be with a woman. Many times, he views the woman as just a bad form of the pornography, an imperfect form of the pornography that he's been using. So he's not more of a man because of pornography. *He is less*.

We want to think that our wives are talking at coffee with their friends saying, "You know, my husband is a wonderful sexual partner." But many times men are failures because of what pornography has done to them.

> *Steve Arterburn is the founder of New Life Ministries, helping men and women to overcome addictions and unhealthy behaviors through nationwide New Life Treatment Centers. He hosts the nationally syndicated* New Life Live *radio program. His books include* Every Man's Battle: Winning the War on Sexual Temptation One Victory at a Time.

We control 50 percent
of a relationship. We influence
100 percent of it.

—Anonymous

There are "friends" who destroy
each other, but a real friend sticks
closer than a brother.

—Proverbs 18:24 [NLT]

9 The Passion of Relationships

Men at times confuse intimacy with sex. But true intimacy is openness and honesty with another person. And the greatest barrier to intimacy is the fear of rejection. People are unwilling to reveal who they really are when they don't feel safe. In contrast, when you are able to be transparent with someone who still accepts you and loves you as a friend, you feel a powerful sense of freedom.

I once interviewed Jerry Biederman, author of *Secrets of a Small Town.* Biederman had visited a small town (which he would not identify) and met with a number of people who volunteered their "secrets" to him. They did so under the complete assurance that he would never reveal the town or any identifying characteristics of their story. That was the basis for his book.

I was amazed at the things the townspeople told Biederman. I was amazed on two levels. Some people felt great guilt over tiny, small offenses. One person was living with the guilt of going into the father's bedroom and looking in his dresser without permission. The guilt of that action lasted for years! But some townspeople confessed to major crimes. Biederman told me that one person confessed to a murder—a crime that had never been solved!

Finding Someone to Hear a Secret

The intrigue of this interview for me was in listening to the author explain how people longed for someone with whom they could share their secrets. But not just anyone. It had to be someone they could trust. And yet, even though these small-town confidants had never met this author before, they were willing to provide their most hidden moments. Why?

The answer, I believe, is twofold. First, people have a need to "clear the conscience." Self-revelation in essence says, "OK. It's out there. Finally!" But the second reason is what I stated earlier. Somewhere out there, we hope to find a friend who will hear our worst offense and still accept us! And perhaps the "revealers" also feel safe because their confessions are to a stranger who they will never see again.

Two years later I conducted another radio interview about secrets we keep, this time with Patrick Means, author of *Men's Secret Wars*. At the end, I asked if there were men listening who were living with a secret that was deeply troubling them. If so, and they wanted to meet and share that secret with someone who would not condemn them and could still accept them as a person, I would be willing to be that person.

I did receive three calls after that radio interview, and I met with two of these men separately over lunch.

Two Freeing Admissions

Toward the end of the first lunch, the first man eventually admitted that he had molested his children, even though he had denied it to his pastor. I advised him over lunch that if he wanted to be truly free, he needed to admit his wrongdoing to his family . . . and to his pastor . . . and to the legal authorities, as this would become a legal mat-ter. Then I suggested that if he wanted to take his freedom to the next level, he should consider sharing his story with me *on the radio* at some point in the future.

To my utter amazement, this man did everything we discussed. It cost him everything you could imagine, including time in jail. It cost him his marriage and relationships with his children. And perhaps it cost his health—he eventually developed cancer. Later, he actually ap-peared on my radio program anonymously admitting to his worst moral failure.

Did he experience freedom? Of course he did! When a man re-veals his deepest, darkest secret that exposes his weakness, he is com-pletely vulnerable. But at that point, there is nothing left to worry about. It's done. The terror grip of being discovered is removed. Free, at last.

The second man, a banker in his late twenties, seemingly had a far less complex situation. Our lunch at a Denny's restaurant began with pleasantries about his work. Eventually I turned the conversa-tion to ask, "What is it you would like to talk about?" He struggled to get his story in the open. So I set the stage by saying, "Well, did you murder someone? Did you embezzle or rob a bank?" He quickly said no. *But the shame of what he was going to share was just as intense as if he had done those things.*

He finally admitted that he was struggling with homosexuality. And here is what he expected to happen with that revelation. He anticipated what most men might do. A raised eyebrow. A look of consternation and judgment. A wagging finger of criticism telling him to get his act together. But he would not get that from me.

The reason I could not be his judge is because I have come to grips with my own sin. And it is greater than even I understand. How could I stand in judgment on either of these two men when I know I have harbored thoughts and committed acts of lying, deception, mistruth, fantasies, and such myself? Recognizing our own weakness causes us to be challenged by the words of Jesus when He says, "Physician, heal thyself!"

Instead, I just simply created a safe environment where these men could be open and honest about their greatest weakness (as they perceived it) and find a soul who could accept them. The second man didn't want to be homosexual; he knew it was wrong. But the battle was getting more intense. Cruising neighborhoods. Internet activity. A private thought-life he could not control. This man went on to deal with his personal hell, and while his "tendencies" have not fully abated, he has been able to manage his situation.

Every man has a passion for relationships, and genuine relationships are built on intimacy.

Intimacy and Your Parents

So where does intimacy begin? It should begin at home. And for men, it should begin with our fathers. To know that we are loved and accepted by our earthly fathers is very important to a boy. Getting to know about how a man thinks and what he believes are key to intimacy. A healthy relationship with your father nurtures an even more critical relationship, one with your heavenly Father. God has created us with intimacy in mind. He is a personal God whose nature and heart reaches out. He wants us to know Him and He wants to know us.

Having a father who you believe cares about you as "the most important person" would logically suggest this would be a person you could talk to. Most fathers want their sons to feel they can be trusted. I always wanted my boys to feel they could discuss anything with me. And I wanted them to know they were fully accepted and loved.

The fatherly love of God is manifested in the most dramatic fashion by the presence on this earth of Jesus of Nazareth. While appearing to the interested parties of His day as being but flesh, the reality they learned was that Jesus was much more than that. His incredible story is available for all to read in the gospels of Matthew, Mark, Luke, and John in the Bible. What should not be missed in the life of Jesus is His choosing of twelve men to be His trusted friends, and three of them to be His closest. Jesus developed friendships with men as the divine Son of God! He is all about relationship.

Family relationships should prepare you in other ways as well. A man's relationship to his mother enables him to see a woman in a special way. It has been said that watching the way a man treats his mother will reveal how a man will treat his wife. I don't know if that is universally true but it bears mentioning. If a boy has a mother who loves and accepts him and is always looking after him, he is more prone to look for a woman who cares about him in such a tender and committed fashion.

Intimacy and Your Wife and Children

My relationship with Rhonda is approaching thirty years, and we're still talking with each other! In fact, she is my best friend. Our relationship sustains itself because of commitment, to be sure, but it grows because we spend much time talking with each other. She is a devoted mother and wife and wants relationship—to know, and to be known.

A man truly passionate about relationships will also treasure those with his children. More than offspring to carry on the family, children bear the imprint of a father. Many a father has allowed time to pass while busily engaged in activities which do not include family. Fathers must build in traditions and memory-making experiences for children to hang on to.

How Men and Women Differ

Why is it that men in particular find it hard to build relationships? Why are women seemingly better at this? I wrote my notes for this chapter while enjoying my morning brew at a neighborhood coffee shop. It was around nine o'clock in the morning. There were about twenty women in the coffee shop. Six of them had brought their kids.

I found myself observing their interaction. Everything they were doing was about relationship.

Now a guy might ask, "Don't they have anything else to do?" Men don't quite get the importance of a woman's relationship drive. Women think relationships *first*. Now, men *do* long for relationships—with a father, a mother, with a good wife, children, and friends. They just have to work harder at getting there.

If you grew up in a home knowing that you were loved and accepted, encouraged and safe, you were off to a great start in life. If your parents visibly loved each other, this was a terrific bonus. That was my situation.

Safety and Intimacy

But I've discovered the single most important relational component in the contest of love is experienced through *safety*. Feeling safe with someone opens the doors of communication and value as a human being. It's the critical piece that has to exist in order for small groups to survive.

How does a relationship become "safe"? The sense of *trust* and *acceptance* are the vital elements. In order to meet the need for relationship safety, people often choose to meet with a group or groups that are defined by similar interests.

Gangs form out of a need for acceptance. The school environment creates subgroups of all kinds based on similar interests. A sense of belonging is very important. Churches are like that as well, sometimes to the detriment of members. But other times it becomes a relationship-building function, such as among young-marrieds or the seniors.

Your Deep Need for Relationships

People form in groups for the purpose of relationship, and a real man needs to be in relationship. Your effectiveness as a man increases when you are able to be a relational being. You're a better lover, father, worker, manager, and friend. For men and women alike, authentic relationships require transparency.

Glenn Murray lives in California and has devoted much of his life to "taking down the net": those barriers that keep people from considering the truth about Jesus of Nazareth. Glenn has mentored me in several areas of life, and in the limited amount of time we have spent together, he has had a profound impact on my life. Glenn fosters relationships with others every day and is responsible for fueling my interest in small groups.

Small groups help to develop our relationship skills. There we can share our victories and defeats. Discussing those defeats are the hard part. Painful memories, insecurities, weaknesses, and failures shape us. We need a place where those can be hashed out for our growth.

By now, our two objectives for this discussion of a man's passions should be imbedded in your mind: creating a sense of belonging in the fellowship of men and finding balance in our passions.

Components of Relationships

Relational Level

The first component in this passion is the *relational level.* The depth of intimacy, that is, the relational level, determines the quality of connectedness. Each relationship you have (excluding your family relationships) begins by taking an interest in others on the surface and social levels. From this first level, a relationship may move to building a friendship, usually around a shared interest. It advances to developing an openness that enables you to really *know* a person. Finally, the deepest relational level is becoming a soul mate where deep matters of the heart are discussed and entrusted. That is true intimacy.

Relational Priorities

Relational priorities are the second component, where you choose which relationships deserve more of your time and energy. You must decide which ones should be the most important and life changing.

The first relationship to be established is an intimate one with your Creator. How is that possible? You can't see, feel, touch, smell, or physically hear Him How *do you* become intimate with God?

God has already determined the process for that. He introduces us to Himself through Jesus. As you get to know Jesus through the Bible and then as you expose your heart to His truths, you engage Him on a personal level. Following the placing of your trust in Jesus as the Son of God who embodies all that God is, you are given the very presence of God in your life through the Holy Spirit. He comes to dwell inside of you. Our time in prayer is an exchange of relationship—letting God know more of us while asking to have more of Him revealed as well.

Most relationships are not made in heaven. They come in kits and you have to put them together yourselves.
■ Unknown

Keep on loving each other as brothers.
■ Hebrews 13:1

The next relational priority ought to be your wife, assuming you are married. God clearly indicated this by saying that in marriage, you and your wife are "one." Where you are, she is! Make her a priority . . . and your children, too.

Your children must be a relationship priority. (If you don't have a wife or children, your close friends next deserve your attention, your loyalty, and your energy.) If your sons and daughters are not priorities, you may lose them either as teens or adults. Harry Chapin made it known to the world in his hit song from several years ago, "Cat's in the Cradle." Chapin wrote and sung of a man whose boy grew up to be "just like me" in an unexpected way—ignoring his father who had ignored him.

Finally comes the priority of having "a few good friends." A few is all a man will likely have in life.

Relational Fundamentals

The third component is called *relational fundamentals*, the factors that determine success or failure in establishing deep and meaningful relationships. The four fundamentals are *trust, acceptance, mutual respect,* and *unconditional love.* You can have acceptance but not necessarily unconditional love for a person. You can have mutual respect while you may not be fully accepting of the other person.

Having all four leads to deeper relationships. When you combine these four relational fundamentals, you have a pretty good opportunity for intimacy.

Relational Risk

Relational risk is the fourth component—the things that put relationships in peril. Foremost among relational risks is the broken trust. Because trust is so important to establish intimacy, a broken trust makes it hard, if not impossible, to reestablish. Conditional acceptance will inhibit relational growth as well. If you experience disappointment in a person's availability or you receive an inappropriate response to something important to you, there is a breach in the relationship.

The final risk is that the relationship becomes a one-way street. If you find out many times that you're initiating and the other person is not, the relationship is becoming one-sided and will suffer; eventually such a relationship will fail.

A man's passion for relationship is among one of the most rewarding of his passions. It is worth every effort of pursuit. Why did God design man with a desire for relationship? Because that is *His* nature. He created us with a free will, which opens the door for the incredible dynamic of love to be expressed.

The Relationship Continuum

The relationship continuum identifies two extremes in relationships. We can be *the hermit* or *the gadabout*, but it is better to be in the middle. On the far left is *the hermit*.

The hermit is the man who claims that he either wants or needs no one. He avoids social interaction. His preference is to be a loner and remain isolated and unattached. You could say he is "forlorn, forsaken, and friendless." Often displaced, he might find himself to be transient, a deserter, or a vagabond. This man might well have walked out on a lot of relationships.

The Relationship Continuum

The Hermit   **The Gadabout**

In Balance

While this is an extreme, if you lean toward the loner tendencies, you may well need a wake-up call on the significance of relationships. Whatever reason you use to justify your independence from serious human interaction, you are missing an important part of God's design for man. Consider Jesus as the example. He certainly found time to be alone but spent His days interacting with people. That is where the action is in God's creation.

At the other end of the continuum is *the gadabout*. He loves to fraternize and mingle. He is always talking to people and having a good old time. But his interests are superficial. Try to go deep with him and he kind of draws the line right there. Depth of relationship is really absent from his life. Instead, he loves to be known, loves to say he has many friends. He can be a rumormonger and a talebearer. He is not a man to be trusted.

The gadabout cheapens the nature of relationships. While he appears to be a "people person" at first glance, he isn't. People are simply social conveniences and not held in high esteem or value. He may be this way because he fears being known, or simply because it is too complex to get to know people. This is not the nature of a godly man either. If you identify with this description, you need to ask God to give you a genuine heart for people. Jesus' heart was always touched by others' pain and the realities of their lives.

You will find that the most meaningful events and memories of life are centered in deep relationships. Pursue them.

Manhood Models

As a young man, *Larry Crabb* struggled with stuttering. He once offered a public prayer in his church under the pressure of the moment. He did not want to pray, and he included a terribly confusing sentence. Later, he vowed he would never speak or pray out loud in front of a group.

However, afterward, one of the elders came up to Larry and, instead of chiding him or being critical, offered him full support. The elder's words made a lifelong impact on his ministry.

Today, professor and counselor Larry Crabb helps men (and women, too) with such books on relationships as *The Pressure's Off, The Marriage Builder, Men and Women,* and *The Silence of Adam.* His life is about relationships . . . how to mend them and how to keep them intact. Larry has expressed his concern about men who as boys felt neglected by their dads, noting that these men often remain distant from their own children. It is a form of self-protection that results from the "sins of father."

According to Dr. Crabb, men run from feeling the hurt because of unmet longings that come from a lack of deeper relationships. As a result, the efforts made to love appear more like required action than by liberating passion.

No men are better models of honesty in relationships than Larry Crabb, who is highly transparent about himself in all his writings, and the elder of the church, who saw the heart and honesty of Larry and commended the young man for it, thus launching a lifelong ministry for Crabb.

Todd Wilson was raised by a Christian family and turned his heart toward God at an early age. During his junior year at Purdue University, however, he committed himself fully to God, saying, "I've run the first twenty years. You've got the rest." Later he received his master of divinity degree from Grace Theological Seminary and became a pastor. Then, after twelve years, he quit.

> *You can't stay in your corner of the forest waiting for others to come to you. You have to go to them sometimes.*
> ■ Winnie the Pooh

But for the right reasons. He wanted to help other fathers and his almost-overwhelmed wife.

Todd and Debbie have seven children. If the five boys and two girls don't keep Mom busy enough, add to that Debbie's homeschooling of the five older children. Todd now assists his wife by teaching at home, usually a day a week.

He gave up his steady income as a pastor in northern Indiana to devote himself to a ministry that would encourage and help dads, husbands, and families. Through speaking, writing, and modeling a husband who helps a wife, Todd is helping other fathers to become leaders of their families.

Today he leads Familyman Ministries and publishes an Internet column, "Familyman Weekly," which is e-mailed to thousands of men each week. His ability to laugh at himself and at the challenges every man faces as a father make for fun and welcomed reading. *Christianity Today* now posts "The Familyman Weekly" column on its Web site.[1]

Through his free e-newsletter and speaking to dads, he urges men to do what they are called to do—being good fathers and husbands. Todd is all about men and their most important relationships.

Wired for Relationships

If pursuing relationships is difficult for you, here are two areas where you can begin. Learn to appreciate and enjoy those you meet day by day. A man who knows how to truly enjoy people, to sense their needs, and to help them fulfill their dreams is a man whom other men will want as their friend. Second, if you are married, learn about your wife and your children. Maybe you need to devote more energy to family time. A man who does not have enough time to learn about his wife or his kids is too busy.

You are wired as a man for relationship. How do I know that? Because God created you in His image and He loves relationships. With that embracing love that God has for you, He, in turn, is asking you to "Go . . . and do likewise." Remember, when you find one or two men to share your world in complete safety, you have a treasure untold.

Takeaways

Relationship, like the other passions of a man, is a God-given part of life. Here are some guidelines in using this gift from God.

■ *A fundamental question to ask yourselves is, "Do I need other people?" If the answer is no, you are relationally challenged.* That may seem a harsh statement, but the response to the question is harsh indeed! God has truly constructed the human race as a group of interdependent people. We are made to be part of a family, each contributing something of value to each other.

- *Relationship building is a cultivated skill.* It requires us to consciously move from self-interest to an interest in others. This is what makes relationships *work.* They do not happen all by themselves. It takes interested and concerned parties. As you develop a growing interest in others, you will find that this gets reciprocated in wonderful, fulfilling ways.

- *The greater the degree of vulnerability shared in an accepted environment, the greater the sense of personal freedom we achieve.* The two men who met with me over lunch confirm this truth. Becoming a transparent person with that trusted friend enables you to find great freedom in accepting who you are. And it opens the door for an exchange of such honesty. It also breaks down barriers for others to love you as a real person, not some pretending saint.

- *The biggest surprise we find in true intimacy with another person is how common our true fears, worries, and wrongdoings are shared by another person.* That's really the beauty of being transparent. Years ago I struggled with phobias and panic attacks. My greatest relief came when I overheard someone at a Bible study group share a similar burden. In fact, it brought back a sense of normalcy to my life. As you hear of others who struggle and deal with the similar issues you face, it opens the door for deep conversation and friendships. Of course, you must be willing to make those same kinds of things known.

- *Developing intimacy skills brings us closer to our humanity and our need for a redeemer.* Your soul gets a workout with God when you are able to be your true self. It is often said about radio personalities that the most difficult challenge they face is to learn to be *themselves.* How often do you mask or portray a person who is not really you? In the spiritual sense, this will always fail in front of the God who made you. He already knows who you are . . . inside and out. By confessing your most intimate thoughts to Him, you create the kind of relationship that God wants to use to help you grow.

Principles . . . of Relationships

Here are three key principles on relationships to keep in mind:

1. *It is up to you to create the "safe place" in a relationship.* You do that by affirming in word and deed your willingness to be accepting and trusting of the other person. How is that done? Being intentional about it is a good way to start. Be sure that secrets can be trusted with you. Affirm your willingness to keep private those things told to you in private. And live by that. Let your children know that their world is safe with you and establish this by not overreacting as a parent when things seem to turn in the wrong direction. Spend life proving you are a trusted friend.

2. *Transparency is what opens the door to deeper friendships.* Be selective. Be patient. Some men are naturally more relational. They are also at greater risk of rushing into areas of confidentiality without really knowing the safety level of their sharing partner. In this chapter, I have been encouraging transparency —giving someone the privilege to "look through you." That can be very revealing and, depending on the person, it could be damaging. Share those details carefully and with a limited few.

3. *Your sense of God's presence and His peace is an intimacy issue.* God's heart is very tender to a humble man willing to share it all with Him. How wonderful it is to be a "friend of God."

True friends live out their friendship in tangible ways. If your heart desires to be a friend of God, tell Him so. And begin practicing the effort to know Him more and revealing yourself to Him in greater detail. A friend of God has peace. And an eternal friendship.

Note

1. The free weekly column can be found at http://www.christianitytoday.com/men and at http.//www.familymanweb.com.

Insights on Relationships
. . . *with Gary Chapman*

Few people are naturally gifted at building relationships. I think the art of building strong relationships is a "learned phenomenon."

For close relationships and friendships, one of the most important words is *openness*. With the right person, we can be very open; we can share honestly our thoughts and feelings. By nature, many of us men tend to hold our thoughts and feelings close to ourselves. We're not as free to open up. In a genuine friendship there will be a sense of openness, a willingness to share our struggles, our thoughts, and our feelings. There also will be a genuine sense of caring for the other person. You are willing to do things to help the other person, and if it's a real friendship it's a reciprocal thing. You both are there for each other.

Our experiences with relationships can affect our relationship with God. If a man tends to be rather withdrawn from people because he senses that people would not like him, he might also carry that over into his relationship with God. He may feel that God would not like him if God really knew him. Of course, God does. On the other hand, I think there are examples of people who do not relate to people very well but they have a deep and intimate relationship with God. In a sense, they have learned to be comfortable in sharing their hearts with God but they never learned to be comfortable in sharing their hearts with people.

I recommend two resources to men trying to develop better relationship skills. Patrick Morley's classic, *The Man in the Mirror*, has a section on relationships that is very helpful. The book deals with relationships in a way that a lot of men have found very helpful. My book *The Five Love Languages: Men's Edition* is written specifically to help men with the relationship with their wives. It has implications in one chapter that relates to their children. For a married man, that's probably the place to start in enhancing his relationships—with his wife and children. Those same skills spill over into other relationships.

If a man has really had a difficult time in relationships most of his life, he can change and develop relationships. We can all change. In fact, we are changing every day. We're changing either for the better or for the worse. A man who as an adult comes to know Christ and opens his mind and his heart to Christ, to the Scriptures, and the Holy Spirit can change in a very positive way. It will not only change his inner character but also his relationship to people.

Whatever your past has been, with the help of God you can make tremendous strides in learning how to have good relationships. If you're meeting with a men's group or one-on-one with another man, you will also find that to be extremely encouraging.

Gary Chapman is a gifted marriage counselor and marriage seminar leader. His books The Five Love Languages, The Five Love Languages of Singles, *and other books in the Love Languages series have sold more than 4.5 million copies.*

We succeed only as we identify in life, or in war or in anything else, a single overriding objective, and make all other considerations bend to that one objective.

—Dwight Eisenhower

■

*He has showed you, O man, what is good. And what does the L*ORD *require of you? To act justly and to love mercy and to walk humbly with your God.*

—Micah 6:8

10 The Passion of Legacy

As my employer, he gave me a most unusual assignment: Take a day off. Well, it wasn't quite that simple. I was to take a day off for some *deep*, *personal analysis*. Oooohh. Sounds heavy. And it was.

I was given a rather interesting challenge. My boss was a friend. He believed I was at a point in my life where I might really benefit from an intense day of introspection. I would create, in essence, a "top secret" personality dossier on Mark Elfstrand.

Many men might have viewed this in different ways. You could feel uncomfortable with heavy introspection and ask, "What kind of an assignment is that?" Another man might have felt it was meddling for an employer to suggest that a man needed to do such a thing. A third response might have been to consider that assignment a mystery. Exactly where do you start in giving your life an honesty checkup? But I readily accepted the challenge.

I knew my friend wanted to help me and serve my best interest; getting me to a new level of personal discovery was his goal.

I picked the day and got in my car and drove to an isolated spot in western Pennsylvania near Pittsburgh where we lived. It had a "cheap motel" in town, so I checked in early in the morning as a day guest. I had brought my computer with me. The work began.

Most of that day was spent writing. Then thinking. And writing some more. Then praying for a while, asking God to reveal through this exercise something that would be of lasting value to me. I was giving my life a very introspective evaluation. I wrote things down that I didn't want anyone else to see.

Along with trying to define with some precision the makeup of myself as a person, I spent a good portion of the day considering some life questions. Where am I going? Did my life really matter so far? How can I make it matter before it's over?

I went home and printed the results and placed them in a red folder. No one else had seen these notes. There is something about deep soul transparency that a man needs to keep private. While I know that God was aware of all these details, and more, I was not and am not willing to make them public in any form. In fact, I have often thought about destroying this file, except that it serves me well to occasionally review what I wrote.

So what difference did this exercise make in my life? I will not say it was one of the most profound, life-changing events of my life. But it required of me something which most men do not want to do: take inventory. Men find themselves with this dichotomy. We want to know that our lives made a difference on this earth, and yet we are afraid to ask the questions that give us the answers to our true value. We fear the answer might be, "Not much."

In this final chapter I'm going to address the issues related to your life value. The term for this is *legacy*. It is what you leave behind that others remember about you. Legacy is your *personal imprint* on this world.

In the movie *Jerry McGuire*, Jerry (played by Tom Cruise) is thirty-five years old and a professional sports agent. He experiences an early midlife career crisis. On an evening when he cannot seem to fall asleep, he does some self-analysis. We are given a glimpse of his thoughts as he reveals, "I couldn't escape one simple thought. I hated myself. No, no; here's what it was. I hated my place in the world."

Jerry McGuire had what some call a *kairos* experience. This is a Greek word meaning the "right or opportune moment." He set out to write a mission statement, staying up all night. He admits in his hour of self-examination that with so many clients, his company had forgotten what was important. Like my day set aside for personal review, Jerry McGuire wrote all night. He developed a new strategy, one that would be centered on caring for others. It is a radical point of self-discovery when he realizes "this was the 'me' I always wanted to be."

Three Stages of Life

I think a man's first twenty-five years of life are about discovery and having fun. That would be the legacy of his short life. (Of course, this only applies to affluent cultures. In many parts of the world, a young man is only concerned with survival and getting the next meal.) During these early years, we're very concerned about *image*.

Between age twenty-five and fifty, *recognition*, *respect*, and *reputation* become very important words for a man. We seek to prove our worthiness on the job and in social circles by our achievements and by our lifestyle. Performance is the measurement device we use to determine our legacy.

After age fifty, a different thinking process occurs. A man now comes to grips with the reality that he is well into the second half of life. He is forced to look at what he has really accomplished. Did it matter? How much time does he have left? What will make it worthwhile? How *will* he be remembered? Said another way, he might be asking, "What monument would represent my life?"

Those three stages of life reflect three quests in developing our legacy: our image, reputation, and monuments. Most of what determines our legacy is constructed from what our motivations in life have been—what lasting monuments (if any) we are building. Over time, people can discern the kind of person you are by watching you in action and seeing what truly motivates you.

Three Kinds of Coaches

In his book *Second Wind from the Second Half,* Patrick Morley compares men with such goals to three different kinds of coaches. For one coach, it's very important to build confidence in his ballplayers. The win/loss record is important, but that's not really who he is or what he is about. He's about building character in his players.

The second kind of coach works on winning. It is almost everything. If you are one of his players, you give it all. You pour yourself into your work; you focus on being a winner. That's what's important.

A third coach has a different kind of passion, Morley writes. This coach's ambition may be to help the greatest number of underprivileged kids find a full or partial scholarship. His job satisfaction comes from the pleasure of helping others.

You will make your own decision on whether each is equally as valid and the kind of coaching style that most represents your life. Teaching confidence and character is important. Developing champions who pursue excellence is a noble thing. Helping kids get scholarships is certainly a noteworthy objective. Which one will be remembered most? And for what reason? To me, the issue of motivation surfaces again. Did the coach do it all for his glory . . . or does his legacy prove something else?

It might be good right now to consider that question as it applies to you. To this point in your life, is your legacy one of service and people building? Or would others say it was about creating your personal empire and reputation? No doubt every life has acts of kindness or goodness to be remembered, but what will people be able to say about you at your funeral . . . and beyond? That is legacy.

A King's Legacy

One of the most eerie and disturbing biblical stories calling a man to account for his life appears in Daniel 5. Belshazzar, king of Babylon, is enjoying a big feast, but outside the palace the Persian army is waiting, planning to take over his country. In the midst of this banquet, the fingers of a human hand mysteriously appear and begin to write on the wall. To say the least, King Belshazzar is terrified. No one can interpret the writing.

The queen suggests that the king call in Daniel, a young Jewish exile whose insight, intelligence, and wisdom had been clearly established. The king seeks his counsel.

Daniel boldly tells King Belshazzar that the king has set himself up against the Lord of heaven. The inscription reads, *"Mene, mene, tekel, parsin."* Daniel interprets this message as follows: "God has numbered the days of your reign and brought it to an end. . . . You have been weighed on the scales and found wanting. . . . Your kingdom is divided and given to the Medes and Persians" (Daniel 5:26–28).

> *Be more concerned with your character than your reputation, because your character is what you really are, while your reputation is merely what others think you are.*
> ■ John Wooden

King Belshazzar's legacy at that point is in seriously bad shape. *The Lord of the entire universe has found him wanting.* What if your life review came up before the Lord today? Suppose you opened your e-mail and found such a challenge? Would it be said of you that your life review was complete and that God *found it wanting*?

This is the question we must address as we look at a man's passion for legacy. We live on earth for a reason: God desires to manifest Himself in us. While image and reputation are important, at some point in our lives we must realize that what really matters is what we leave behind.

The *Cambridge Dictionary* defines legacy as something which is a part of your history or which stays from an earlier time. It is, in essence, a gift that is left for those who remain after one leaves. If you have a desire to make such an impact in life, you are thinking like a man. If you are going to pursue this passion, you need to know what it means to be in balance in your quest.

Components of a Legacy

The Purpose Statement

The first component of a legacy is a *purpose statement.* The purpose statement is really *a personally crafted description of how you intend for your life to have meaning.* President Dwight Eisenhower defined success as knowing and fulfilling that intention (or objective): "We succeed only as we identify in life, or in war or in anything else, a single overriding objective, and make all other considerations bend to that one objective."

Do you have one overriding objective yet? Years ago, I discovered in a book about writing business plans a quote that is profound but almost absurd in simplicity: "If you cannot describe something in clear terms, you have not thought it through sufficiently." I am in the communications business. We can make the simple incredibly complex.

The test for simplicity is to run it past someone who has never seen the item before. If the person "gets it" on the first round, you have probably succeeded. Your purpose statement for life should be clear enough for others to *identify* with it. (One of the finest resources for men along these lines is The Great Adventure video study series, complete with DVD and study guide from Men's Fraternity.)

A purpose statement forces the issue—you are meant to have purpose. It enables you to stay on course.

A Set of Values

The second component is a *set of values.* These values are derived from your moral compass. This is the belief system that drives the motivations that, in turn, guide the way you live your life. Great leaders are men of conviction and belief. Deep convictions ought to be built on truth. You need to have a source of moral truth.

This is the age of relativism, when values tend to shift with differing circumstances. A well-developed moral foundation doesn't allow for that. Your willingness to stand for the principles that you embrace will impact future generations as well.

Impact Criteria

The next component of a legacy is the *impact criteria*, your perspective on the most important areas of life that you can transfer to make an imprint on the life of others. This is different than a set of values. Here is where you ask, "Exactly what *do* I want to pass along to my family?" It's something tangible, and can range from a recorded history to a recipe book and even a financial gift.

I am on the planning team for a leadership event known as the Chicago Executive Forum. One of the men on our Board of Reference recently completed a superb project: *individual books* written for his grandchildren. Each of these books contains a fair amount of material in common. Grandpa tells a lot about his personal history, including stories about his dad (their great-grandfather) and what it was like to grow up in his family. He shares key events in his life that shaped him and some of the lessons he has learned in life. You can be assured it took him many hours to complete this.

My wife, Rhonda, did something similar with family recipes one Christmas. She created a family cookbook with the favorite meals our family has enjoyed over the years. It's almost 180 pages of recipes, complete with pictures. What a treasure! Those are legacy builders.

Leaving part of your legacy behind involves sharing who you are, the experiences that determined why you are the way you are, and the principles that you hold dearly. This does not need to be a book but perhaps some thoughts simply crafted on paper.

Another way to make a legacy impact is financial. Family foundations are often set up for this express purpose. Moody Publishers offers several financial resources but one worth noting here is the book, *Splitting Heirs.* Contributions to cultural or social organizations are another way that your values become part of your impact criteria for a lasting legacy.

Method of Evaluation

The last component of legacy, *a method of evaluation*, helps you determine whether your life is staying on course. One of those tools is an internal evaluation. For me, that's my red folder. It's a deep gut check of who I am and why I am the way I am—and what I plan to be doing about it.

Another method is an external evaluation. It's building your own small board of directors and asking them to take a look at your life and challenge you with the hard questions. Your board doesn't have to convene formally, of course, but you may decide to meet one time a year and review your life purpose. Usually around the first of the year is a good time to do this kind of review.

If you want to be a man of impact, you need to apply these legacy components. A man's passion for legacy is the most *enduring* of his passions. It will take disciplined thinking and action to make the desired impact. Why did God design man with a desire for legacy? Because God created man with His own divine imprint. He is the God of eternity who offers us the opportunity to spend that eternity with Him. His values are eternal. Ours need to be as well.

The Legacy Continuum

The passion of legacy continuum provides quite a contrast! At one end there is *the black sheep*, the least reputable member of a group. This is the family member no one wants to mention. His life includes acts or a lifestyle that brings disrespect on the family name.

Perhaps your life has been like this. In your past, there are details which you wish you could wipe out. But you know you can't. This does not need to be your legacy, however. It may forever be *part* of your legacy, but not the defining moments. Your commitment to embrace noble values at this stage of your life and to act on those values can bring about a turnaround story that God can use in wonderful ways. Tell Him you want that kind of legacy. Seek out men who will help you move in that direction.

The Legacy Continuum

The Black Sheep   **The Idol**

In Balance

At the other end of our continuum is *the idol*. He lives to be idolized, to be known, praised, and honored in the public square. Selfish interests dominate his desire to be remembered. It is tempting to pick on Hollywood types as examples for this but any man may live in this way. Media stars are photographed, interviewed, and the minutest details of their existence are publicized. You can easily conclude that these must be the gods of our age, worthy of our attention and worship. We can often find ourselves embracing lifestyles and attitudes of those who are in the limelight.

A true hero performs acts of service or character. For the idol, however, most actions are performed for image-building purposes. Such men are conscious about how they will be remembered—not for gracious acts but for ego's sake. The idol mentality wants a statue, some form of public acclaim, recognizing his importance.

Does this describe you to some degree? Are you looking for ways to keep your name alive for the sake of self-interest? If so, confess this to God and ask Him to revise your life mission statement and remove your name from the place where His belongs.

The man of true worth brings honor to the family name. He is known for his genuine qualities, his moral character, and his life of virtue. That is the man in balance.

Manhood Models

Crawford Loritts Sr. grew up the youngest of fourteen children in a farming family that needed most of the kids to help feed and tend the animals. One Sunday afternoon he received a spanking when, seeing the preacher and other adult guests finish all the chicken before the kids were invited to eat, Crawford exclaimed loudly about the preacher, "He ate the last piece of chicken!"

But Crawford would leave a mighty legacy with his own three children. The youngest, Crawford Jr., would become a associate director of U.S. ministries at Campus Crusade for Christ, and chairman of the board of trustees of Columbia International University.

Talk to Crawford Loritts Jr. and he will describe his father's actions that led to a godly legacy: attending church as a family, having meals always together (Crawford Sr. made sure his children did not wait until the adults had eaten), hosting friends and relatives at the dinner table, and learning to appreciate hard work. Crawford Sr. was a gifted athlete who played in the old Negro Leagues before African-Americans could join Major League Baseball, so he also had to work in the coal mines to earn enough to live. During Crawford's first year of marriage, an explosion in a Virginia coal mine blinded one eye. That ended his baseball career. Later he would work more than thirty years at an A&P warehouse, helping prepare foodstuffs for shipping to the grocery stores.[1]

Crawford Jr. attributes who he is to his father *and* the men before him:

As younger kids, we did things as a family. It was a value of Pop's. He didn't get it from seminars or books. . . . He got it from his father. Where did his father get it from? Well, he got it from his father, Peter, who was a slave who had faith in Christ Jesus, a love for his family, and a desire to reach out and touch generations to come.

Then Crawford Jr. says of his great-grandfather, Peter, that rarely a week goes by when he does not think about Peter, whose legacy endures generations later:

I never met [Peter]. We can't find his grave when we visit the old cemetery . . . yet I sometimes believe that I stand on his shoulders. The blessings that I've received in ministry, the opportunities, the platform, the recognition; I believe all these things are due to that man's prayers setting the prayers of many others in motion.[2]

The legacy of a loving family was passed from one generation to the next.

It's easy to make a buck. It's a lot tougher to make a difference.
■ Tom Brokaw

I have fought the good fight, I have finished the race, I have kept the faith.
■ 2 Timothy 4:7

Another model of legacy is *Robert Lewis*, who has served as directional leader and teaching pastor at the Fellowship Bible Church in Little Rock, Arkansas, since 1980. He also serves as chairman of the board for Fellowship Associates, a church consulting and leadership training program.

His greatest passion is to help men discover the biblical principles of authentic manhood. Following his original invitation for the men of his church to get involved in learning about authentic manhood, attendance in the men's gatherings increased sixfold.

In 1990 he founded Men's Fraternity (www.mensfraternity.com); today his video series The Quest for Authentic Manhood is taught at men's groups in churches around the country. The outreach of this group has been worldwide in a number of settings including churches, college campuses, and prison cell blocks.

Robert Lewis is passionate about seeing these fathers passing along these same principles to their sons. His book *Raising a Modern Day Knight* explains how to do that. What is Robert Lewis's legacy? Call it preserving manhood.

My Purpose Statement . . . and Yours

In planning for a legacy, remember to develop your life-purpose statement, sometimes known as a personal mission statement. Such a statement forces us to narrow our focus on where we plan to prioritize the activities of our lives. There is no shortage of demands on a man's time. Only one person can determine who and what gets that time. That person is you.

One of the best ways to get a grasp on a life-purpose statement is to ask your friends to evaluate your life to this point. Based on their input, determine how you plan to change the negatives to positives and how you will develop the positives you possess to even greater heights.

In writing this manuscript, I have also refined my personal mission statement. Let me share it with you: *To use my communication and creativity skills to build relationships and create resources that help foster personal growth.*

The intersecting of several events in my life has revealed to me the importance of men learning to be men. First, they have to believe they belong with other men. If these passions resonated with you, you belong. Second, I was taught years ago that a man must put forth serious effort to stay in balance. We have all witnessed out-of-control men in our world. It isn't pretty.

Final Thoughts

Here are a couple of final thoughts, one about midcourse corrections, the other about the nature of a lasting legacy:

1. *A man who examines his life with some frequency and makes adjustments is well ahead of most men.* Making course corrections is a part of golf, sailing, and just about any sport. Why not life? This is what keeps us on track.

2. *A lasting legacy is not about fame, fortune, or phenomenal accomplishments. It is about living with character, serving others, and loving God.* Sounds almost too basic, doesn't it? But it is work for a man to do this.

I believe that if Jesus had chosen this century for His earthly ministry, you would have found Him a man of profound thinking and influence. Had He come to your town, you would have made it a point to hear what He had to say. Whether you believed He was the actual Son of God is quite different. I hope you can appreciate Jesus for what He has brought to all mankind. At a minimum, He was the greatest teacher who ever lived.

May your life be blessed with an honorable pursuit of manhood. And may Jesus be your Guide.

Takeaways

Men who seek to leave a legacy should remember these points:

■ *Intentionality in legacy means making some hard evaluations about where your life has been, where it is now, what you want your life to become, and how you want to be remembered.* I've heard it suggested that the best way for a man to approach the "next phase" of life is to determine what he wants to *be* instead of what he wants to *do*. If you buy into that, then determine the man you want to be. Start on that path today.

■ *Because determining your legacy is a process that requires review, accurate assessment, and strategic thought, treat it with the respect that process thinking deserves.* In other words, make time for this important aspect of legacy. Don't rush into it. Don't attempt to produce a life-purpose statement in five minutes. Legacy thinking is a process. Take some time with it.

■ *Getting counsel in the matter of what is important and what is worthwhile for your life is a good thing. Start with the Holy Spirit.* Even people of faith fail to appreciate the work of God's gift to His followers. Jesus promised that the very essence of God would dwell inside of us. He is known as the Holy Spirit and is our Counselor. The more intimate you are in the relationship with God, the more you are able to sense His presence through the way that He directs you either to do something or not to do something.

■ *Your intent is not to be idolized or hero-worshiped.* At least it should not be. Your objective is to live a life worth remembering. Develop a clear mind-set about what the difference is. Demand of yourself that you put aside the self-seeking nature.

Principles . . . of Legacy

Here are a few final principles as you seek to develop a meaningful legacy:

1. *You* will be remembered *when you leave this earth.* It may be for a short or long time, for good or for evil. It may be for greatness or weakness, for living for self or for others. You make the call. I think this is one of the most difficult concepts for men to live with on a day-by-day basis. Much of what we do is focused on the short-term and getting the job done. We fail to reflect on the impact of long-term considerations. That is what legacy thinking does.

2. *Your monument will depend a lot on your motivation.* Among the self-examination issues, make your motivation a priority one. The importance of motivation was discussed in the very first chapter on purpose. It cannot be understated. A man's hidden motives are who the *true man* is. It is a difficult thing to always have pure motives. Examine yours often.

3. *A journal or written evidence of your life and what matters to you will be a powerful resource in legacy thinking.* Most men of greatness have kept a journal. I attended a radio function where this was brought out. Journal keeping is apparently one of three significant growth tools used by the majority of gifted leaders. It makes sense. You learn from your experiences!

Notes

1. Crawford W. Loritts Jr., *Never Walk Away* (Chicago: Moody, 1997), 49–58.

2. Ibid., 58–59.

Insights on Leaving a Legacy
. . . with Crawford Loritts

Most men need to think about their "life impact." Instead, most of us have become concerned about our kids, our jobs, and paying our bills—the daily stuff. We get pulled into just the function side of life in greeting the pressures of everything before us.

Sometime between age forty and sixty, that twenty-year window when the kids are getting older, we realize that we're losing some of the energy we had in our youth. We start regretting certain things. Up until that time we don't spend a lot of time doing that.

I think the best way of getting a good handle on who you are and what is most important in life is to surrender to the lordship of Jesus Christ. A man needs to realize that God has a plan for all of life. He has made us for a purpose, and we need to surrender to Him. Second, we need to surround ourselves with other brothers in Christ who love us and who love the Lord. They can give us some objectivity about ourselves. Third, we need to be sure that we're ministering to others. As we surrender to the lordship of Christ and live in community with other people, then we're actively involved in expressing the hope and the love of Jesus Christ to people around us. It gives us a sense of gratitude, of purpose, of meaning and context.

To begin thinking more clearly about leaving a legacy, I recommend reading biographies of great men and women who have been significantly used of God in their generation. To see the variety of people that God uses gives us all hope—and that's a very important thing. Going to men's conferences that are biblically based also is very helpful. That is where godly men come together to speak on these issues related to our pilgrimage as men.

What timeless values should you focus on passing to the next generation? I think every man wants his kids to do better than he did. My father used to say this all the time. I remember when I was a kid growing up I would get cross with Dad a little bit or do something that I shouldn't do or got off the script, so to speak. He would say to me, "You know Son, let me remind you of something. I am working hard and doing the best I can so that you will go to a place that I can't go to."

The most important thing that we can give to our kids is our own broken, surrendered heart to the Lord Jesus. I just keep coming back to that. Building a godly heritage is not the product of a bank account. Neither is it the product of some genius with a high IQ. But it's all about personal godliness.

In a real sense the whole of the Bible is about legacy. Paul talks about the things that you "heard from me among many witnesses" (2 Timothy 2:2, NKJV). He says commit yourself to that and to teach others also. When Paul is about ready to die he's giving Timothy this charge by making this illustration: "I'm going to receive a crown of righteousness!" (see 2 Timothy 4:8). The context there is a motivational statement: "I completed my course but you still have some more of this track to run. And so if you're going to get what God has in store for me then you need to be faithful in terms of what he's given you to do."

Throughout the Scriptures there is one story after another of passing the baton of righteousness from one generation to the next. That is what legacy is about.

Crawford Loritts Jr. has served Campus Crusade for Christ as a traveling speaker and later as the associate director for Campus Crusade–USA. In addition to serving as a senior pastor, he is the featured speaker on the radio program Living a Legacy.

Recommended Reading

Chapter 1: The Passion for Purpose

Bob Buford. *Half Time.* Grand Rapids: Zondervan, 1997.

Os Guinness. *The Call.* Nashville: W Publishing, 2003.

Gordon MacDonald. *Ordering Your Private World.* rev. ed. Nashville: Nelson, 2003.

Patrick Morley. *The Man in the Mirror.* Nashville: Nelson, 1989.

Rick Warren. *The Purpose-Driven Life.* Grand Rapids: Zondervan, 2002.

Chapter 2: The Passion for Adventure

The Acts of the Apostles. The Bible: various translations.

Stephen E. Ambrose. *Undaunted Courage.* New York: Simon & Schuster, 1996.

John Eldredge. *Wild at Heart.* Nashville: Nelson, 2001.

Mark Twain. *The Adventures of Tom Sawyer.* Various editions.

Tom Wolfe. *The Right Stuff.* New York: Bantam, 2001.

Chapter 3: The Passion for Power

Kevin Belmonte. *Hero for Humanity: A Biography of William Wilberforce.* Colorado Springs: NavPress, 2002.

Lee Ellis. *Leading Talents, Leading Teams.* Chicago: Northfield, 2003.

Hans Finzel. *The Top Ten Mistakes Leaders Make.* Colorado Springs: Cook, 2004.

John C. Maxwell and Jim Dornan. *Becoming a Person of Influence.* Nashville: Nelson, 1997.

Steve Miller. *D. L. Moody on Spiritual Leadership.* Chicago: Moody, 2004.

Joseph M. Stowell. *Perilous Pursuits.* Chicago: Moody, 1994.

Chapter 4: The Passion for Winning

Stephen R. Covey. *The 7 Habits of Highly Effective People.* New York: Free Press, 2004.

Duke Duvall. *How To Conquer Giants.* Sisters: Ore.: Multnomah, 2003.

Stephen Mansfield. *Never Give In: The Extraordinary Character of Winston Churchill.* Nashville: Cumberland, 2002.

Doug McIntosh. *The War Within You.* Chicago: Moody, 2001.

Wess Roberts. *Victory Secrets of Attila the Hun.* New York: Dell, 1994.

J. Steven Wilkins. *All Things for Good: The Steadfast Fidelity of Stonewall Jackson.* Nashville: Cumberland, 2004.

Chapter 5: The Passion for Wealth

Ron Blue and Jeremy L. White. *Splitting Heirs.* Chicago: Northfield, 2004.

Mary Hunt. *The Complete Cheapskate: How to Get out of Debt, Stay Out, and Break Free from Money Worries Forever.* New York: St. Martin's, 2003.

Dave Ramsey. *Financial Peace.* New York: Viking, 1997.

Richard Swenson. *Margin: Restoring Emotional, Physical, Financial and Time Reserves to Overloaded Lives.* Colorado Springs: NavPress, 1995.

Chapter 6: The Passion for Self-Preservation

Neil T. Anderson. *The Bondage Breaker.* Eugene, Ore: Harvest House, 1990.

Larry Crabb, Al Andrews, and Don Michael Hudson. *The Silence of Adam.* Grand Rapids: Zondervan, 1998.

Max Lucado. *Traveling Light.* Nashville: W Publishing, 2001.

Robert S. McGee. *The Search for Significance: Seeing Your True Worth Through God's Eyes.* Nashville: W. Publishing, 2003.

Peter Stark. *Last Breath.* New York: Ballantine, 2001.

James Waldroop and Timothy Butler. *The 12 Bad Habits That Hold Good People Back.* New York: Doubleday, 2001.

Chapter 7: The Passion for the Hunt

Jim Collins. *Good to Great.* New York: Collins, 2001.

Jane A. Kise, David Stark, and Sandra Hirsh. *Life Keys: Discovering Who You Are, Why You're Here, What You Do Best.* Minneapolis: Bethany, 1996.

Tom Paterson. *Living the Life You Were Meant to Live.* Nashville: Nelson, 1998.

C. William Pollard. *The Soul of the Firm.* Grand Rapids: Zondervan, 1996.

Mark Sanborn. *The Fred Factor: How Passion in Your Work and Life Can Turn the Ordinary into the Extraordinary.* Colorado Springs: WaterBrook, 2004.

Chapter 8: The Passion of Pleasure

Steve Arterburn and Fred Stoeker, with Mike Yorkey. *Every Man's Battle.* Colorado Springs: WaterBrook, 2000.

Mark Laaser. *The Secret Sin: Healing the Wounds of Sexual Addiction.* Grand Rapids: Zondervan, 1992.

Timothy Dailey. *Dark Obsession: The Tragedy and Threat of the Homosexual Lifestyle.* Nashville: Broadman & Holman, 2003.

Doug Herman. *Come Clean.* Carol Stream, Ill.: Tyndale, 2004.

Chapter 9: The Passion of Relationships

Gary Chapman. *The Five Love Languages.* Chicago: Northfield, 2004.

Tim and Joy Downs. *The Seven Conflicts: Resolving the Most Common Disagreements in Marriage.* Chicago: Moody, 2003.

Tom L. Eisenman. *The Accountable Man: Pursuing Integrity Through Trust and Friendship.* Downers Grove, Ill.: InterVarsity, 2004.

Randy Frazee. *Making Room for Life: Trading Chaotic Lifestyles for Connected Relationships.* Grand Rapids: Zondervan, 2004.

Mark D. Roberts. *Dare to Be True.* Colorado Springs: WaterBrook, 2003.

Chapter 10: The Passion of Legacy

Phil Downer. *Eternal Impact: Investing in the Lives of Men.* Eugene, Ore.: Harvest House, 1997.

Steve Farrar. *Finishing Strong.* Sisters, Ore,: Multnomah, 2000.

Gordon MacDonald. *Mid-Course Correction.* Nashville: Nelson, 2000.

Bob Reccord and Randy Singer. *Made to Count.* Nashville:W Publishing, 2004.